What people are saying abo

ALL

D0647798

"Brennan's memoir is at once unvarnished and confessional, grippingly honest and poignantly tender. An unguarded peek into a life marked by foibles and blessings, gifts and pain, joy and regret. But always, in every paragraph, grace. Brennan has lived it, experienced it, and grasps the extraordinary power of God's great gift."

Max Lucado, pastor and best-selling author

"Brennan's insistence upon telling the whole truth about his life—and about the grace that has permeated even its most broken places—makes this book not only a page-turner but a life-changer. It is one thing to preach about the unconditional love of our Abba Father; it's quite another to incarnate the truth of that message in the particular pleasures and profound pain of your own deeply personal story. It's tempting to call this book 'brutally honest,' but that's all wrong—it's 'grace-fully honest,' and a very good gift."

Carolyn Arends, recording artist and author

"For as long as I've known him, Brennan Manning has acknowledged that his life is a bundle of paradoxes. By revealing more of his story in his final written work, he strains to convince us that he was telling the truth. Focusing on his shameful flaws and God's incomprehensible grace, this firebrand preacher cries again the message that he's proclaimed for over forty years, that, whether or not you choose to believe it, *All Is Grace.*"

Fil Anderson, author of *Running on Empty* and *Breaking the Rules*

"Brennan Manning has touched many lives, mine included. This poignant memoir reaffirms his truthful message that weakness and failure are not things to be despised but well-lit paths straight into the arms of our Lord."

Ashley Cleveland, three-time Grammy-award winner

"Brennan has always woven bits and pieces of his life's story into his sermons and books. Here, at last, he shares the entire hurtful, redemptive story."

Michael Card, musician and Bible teacher

"Brennan has done it again, offering us a deeply personal book that deals with the brutal honesty of his life's failures and the grace so many fear. It is truly beautiful."

Jay Bakker, copastor of Revolution NYC and author of *Fall to Grace* and *Son of a Preacher Man*

"I count myself among the scores who have been touched by Brennan's life message. He saw life in me when I felt dead, and he was moved by goodness in me when I was bad. Through Brennan, grace is now more real to me. This memoir will make it more real for you."

"While it may very well be Brennan Manning's parting word to us, *All Is Grace* is no deathbed confession. In these soul-stirring pages, Brennan testifies once again of a stubborn, messy grace that does not cleanse us as much as it stains us and marks us forever as one precious to the Most High God. As the old hymn says: *Some through the water, some the floods, some through the fire, but all through the blood … God leads His dear children along.* And, as Brennan shows us in *All Is Grace*, God leads us when we stumble facedown too. *All Is Grace* is the book for all who stumble."

"Brennan once shared with me that you can't compare your insides with everyone else's outsides. This book is a brutally honest look 'behind the curtain' at the man many consider the wizard of spirituality. Whether you're just starting on a spiritual journey or you're on the national speaking circuit, this book is a must-read. I guarantee you'll gain perspective about the pitfalls, the joys, and the ultimate reality of grace in a ragamuffin world."

"This is the bittersweet tale of a great sinner whose appetite for personal destruction is only just eclipsed by his hunger for God. Brennan's transparency is a sweet gift to all who struggle to measure up, or cover up, and a witness to the strength and spaciousness of grace."

Greg Paul, author of *The Twenty-Piece Shuffle*
and *Close Enough to Hear God Breathe*

ALL IS GRACE

A *Ragamuffin* MEMOIR

ALL IS GRACE

BRENNAN MANNING
Best-selling author of *The Ragamuffin Gospel*

WITH JOHN BLASE

David C Cook®
transforming lives together

ALL IS GRACE
Published by David C Cook
4050 Lee Vance View
Colorado Springs, CO 80918 U.S.A.

David C Cook Distribution Canada
55 Woodslee Avenue, Paris, Ontario, Canada N3L 3E5

David C Cook U.K., Kingsway Communications
Eastbourne, East Sussex BN23 6NT, England

Photos courtesy of Art and Geraldine Rubino,
Roslyn Bourgeois, John Krahm, and Rick Christian

LCCN 2011933706
Hardcover ISBN 978-1-4347-6418-8
International Trade Paperback ISBN 978-0-7814-0616-1
eISBN 978-0-7814-0785-4

© 2011 Brennan Manning
Published in association with the literary agency of Alive Communications, Inc.,
7680 Goddard Street, Suite 200,
Colorado Springs, CO 80920, www.alivecommunications.com.

The Team: Don Pape, Nicci Jordan Hubert, Amy Konyndyk,
Nick Lee, Jack Campbell, Karen Athen
Cover Design: Gearbox
Cover Photo: Ben Pearson

Printed in the United States of America
First Edition 2011

2 3 4 5 6 7 8 9 10

091511

for Roslyn

CONTENTS

FOREWORD

I first met Brennan Manning at an event called Greenbelt Festival in England, a sort of Christian Woodstock of artists, musicians, and speakers that had attracted twenty thousand fans to tents and impromptu venues set up in the muddy infield of a horse-racing track. Brennan seemed dazzled by the spectacle, and like a color commentator, kept trying to explain the subtleties of evangelicalism to his wife, Roslyn, a cradle Catholic who lacked Brennan's experience with the subculture.

We did not see each other often over the years, but each time our paths crossed, we went deeper rather than tilling the same

ground of friendship. When he visited a monastery in Colorado
for spiritual retreats, he would sometimes get a temporary dis-
pensation from the rule of silence and meet my wife and me at
an ice-cream parlor (one addiction he doesn't disclose in these
pages). Our backgrounds could hardly have been more different—
Southern fundamentalism versus Northeastern Catholic—and yet
by different routes we had both stumbled upon an artesian well
of grace and have been gulping its waters ever since. One glorious
fall afternoon we hiked on a carpet of golden aspen leaves along
a mountain stream and I heard the details of Brennan's life: his
loveless childhood, his marathon search for God, his marriage
and divorce, his lies and cover-ups, his continuing struggles with
alcohol addiction.

As you read this memoir, you may be tempted, as I was, to
think, *Oh, what might have been … if Brennan hadn't given in to
drink.* I urge you to reframe the thought to, *Oh, what might have
been … if Brennan hadn't discovered grace.* More than once I have
watched this leprechaun of an Irish-Catholic hold spellbound an
audience of thousands by telling in a new and personal way the
story that all of us want to hear: that the Maker of all things loves
and forgives us. Brennan knows well that love and especially the
forgiveness. He may have left the platform that very night for a
hotel room and drunk himself senseless. He admits in these pages
to having broken all Ten Commandments several times over (mur-
der, Brennan?). Each time he begged for forgiveness, repented to
God and to his friends, and got up off the floor to keep walking.
Like Christian, the everyman character in *The Pilgrim's Progress*, he

progressed not by always making right decisions but by responding appropriately to wrong ones. (John Bunyan, after all, titled his own spiritual biography *Grace Abounding to the Chief of Sinners*.)

At one point Brennan likens himself to Samson, that flawed superman whom God somehow found a way to use right up to the day of his death. Reading such stories in the Old Testament, I've come up with a simple principle to explain how God can use the likes of such imperfect men and women: God uses the talent pool available. Again and again, Brennan made himself available. In the last few years, nearly blind, subject to illness and falls, at an age when he should have been enjoying retirement on a beach in Florida, he kept getting on airplanes and flying places to proclaim a gospel he believes with all his heart but has not always lived.

A wealthy man in Denver, having heard Brennan's powerful delivery at a local church, invited him to lead a weeklong retreat for a group of eight handpicked friends, including me. When Brennan announced the retreat would be silent, the benefactor was not happy: "I bring him all the way up here to learn from his expertise, and he wants us to keep silent!" Yet each of us had an hour a day of personal time with Brennan, a compressed time of spiritual direction after meditating on writings and Bible passages he gave us. Brennan worked hard all day while most of the time we sat in the fields or in our rooms and meditated.

Since the camp where we were staying had inadequate facilities, we went each evening to the nearest restaurant, a fancy Chart House. The first night Brennan brought along a boom box with cassette tapes of Rich Mullins and John Michael Talbot, proposing that during dinner we listen to meditative music and continue our time of silence. Soon a chipper waitress showed up. "Hi, guys, how are we all doing tonight?" No response came except for nods and a few tight smiles. A fellow diner recognized one of our group and came over to chat. Patrons at tables around us stared disapprovingly at the boom box, which was pumping out music that blatantly clashed with the restaurant's own Muzak. Brennan laughed, threw up his hands, and made a new rule: silence suspended during evening dinner.

I remember that comical scene when I think of Brennan. More than anyone I know, truly, he has sought a pure and holy life, to the extent of living in a cave in Spain for months, working side by side with the poor, taking vows of chastity, poverty, and obedience. Yet his ideals flounder. Other noises—the clink of wine glasses, laughter from the bar, a woman's voice, distractions from others … in short, the messiness of life—keep interfering with his holy quest. And the inner demons, which no one who has not experienced them can understand, rise up and take control.

"All is grace," Brennan concludes, looking back on a rich but stained life. He has placed his trust in that foundational truth of the universe, which he has proclaimed faithfully and eloquently.

As a writer, I live in daily awareness of how much easier it is to edit a book than edit a life. When I write about what I believe and how I should live, it sounds neat and orderly. When I try to live it out, all hell breaks loose. Reading Brennan's memoir, I see something of the reverse pattern. By focusing on the flaws, he leaves out many of the triumphs. I keep wanting him to tell the stories that put him in a good light, and there are many. Choosing full disclosure in a narrative that might burnish his reputation, Brennan presents himself as the apostle Paul once did, as a clay jar, a disposable container made of baked dirt. We must look to his other books for a full picture of the treasure that lies inside.

A poem by Leonard Cohen says it well:

> *Ring the bells that still can ring.*
> *Forget your perfect offering.*
> *There is a crack in everything.*
> *That's how the light gets in.*

Philip Yancey

READER TESTIMONIES

Have you wondered why God doesn't make your life work or why you can't make your life work? I think we read memoirs hoping that someone has found an answer in his or her own life that can make sense of ours. The pages you are about to read really do lead to an Answer, but your first reaction to these pages might be similar to mine. Initially I was confused, wondering how Brennan could preach a powerful message of grace but live a powerless life of chronic alcoholism. The stories, at first, made me mad—mad at Brennan for being the winsome ragamuffin who relentlessly preached that *"God loves us unconditionally, as we are and not as we*

should be" while living as the reeking-of-vomit drunken ragamuffin who was definitely not as he should be. The promise of this
book—*All Is Grace*—at first struck me as mockery as I read about a
life marked by abuse, betrayal, heartache, addiction, and humiliating illness. The content found in these pages undid me, and then
something completely unexpected and unpredictable happened.

I started to worship.

Confusion turned to gratitude as I began to see that
Brennan's hellish journey of two steps forward, three steps back
kept him so entrenched in a prodigal story that he knew over and
over and over and over again the outlandish grace of the Father
welcoming him home. I, too, have struggled with addiction, and
so Brennan's story helps make sense of my own; but even if you
don't have an addiction, I know you struggle with something
again and again and again. In most testimonies the good news
is only a small part of the story, obscured by our achieving and
overcoming. In Brennan's story, and in mine, the good news is
the entire story, which blessedly leaves us with nothing to prove
or protect.

Allowing Brennan's story to settle deeply into my own turned
anger into trust. Even Brennan's final days with the humiliating
illness of "wet brain" compels me to tell all of my story because
it reveals the certainty of the grace of God—how good He is, not
how bad I am. If we trust grace, we don't need to hide who we
are from one another. Brennan's story invited me to ponder what
it might take for me to tell the unvarnished truth about my life.
Brennan did not need to tell us the dirty details of his alcoholism,

and he certainly did not need to leave us with a final picture of himself as blind, feeble of body and mind, unable to speak clearly or even to take care of himself. He might have rested on his bestseller laurels and finished with one last story of someone impacted by his ministry. Then we could have worshipped him a little and aspired to do something great for Jesus.

Brennan tells his story in a way that strips away everything and leaves us with Jesus. I have faced Him before and felt ashamed or angry, but finding Him at the end of this tale of brokenness really did break me open. And there in the ruins of my own story of dreams and heartache and alcohol and success and marriage and children and divorce and church and ministry and betrayal and forgiveness and love and loss, I saw that it is true, and I worshipped. *It is true.* All is grace.

Sharon A. Hersh, MA, LPC, speaker, and author of *The Last Addiction: Why Self-Help Is Not Enough*

In these pages, Brennan describes a turning moment in his life, a moment in which he spent some three hours lost in a powerful, silent, spiritual *terra incognita* once described by Mircea Eliade as the Golden World. I have known Brennan for many years, but I never heard that story until now.

My own experience of the Golden World began with hearing Brennan speak for about ten minutes once. I arrived late, did not know who he was, and snuck out the back twenty minutes before the end, stunned by a single story he told. All these years later I can still hear him—*"The Father is very, very fond of me."* The experience ended three hours later, with me still unable to speak, Brennan's hands on my shoulders calling me by name though we had never met and my name badge was in my pocket. Like him, I have never told anyone what I heard in my heart that day, but it has made all the difference in my life.

But it is in these pages that I found many things we shared without my knowing it.

It turns out that we both love the Yankees of New York and the eateries of New Orleans. We both discovered the poet James Kavanaugh in his prime and stumbled into Carlo Carretto before Carretto became one of the most famous unknown monks in the world. We each hold one of our grandfathers in high regard simply because they were smart enough to marry the grandmothers we adored. We were both called *just* a dreamer in our lives and figured out a way to take our love for language and wrestle it into a life that only dreamers can live. We have also spent great stretches of our lives struggling with many of the same sorts of demons.

I expect these pages are about to open up some new connections to Brennan for you as well.

You should know that one of the reasons I am actually alive

on this day is because I heard Brennan that long-ago afternoon. To whatever degree I am fully alive today, it is because of what I learned from him.

I learned the truth of the gospel from Brennan, the same gospel you will find in this book: That in the end, my sin will never outweigh God's love. That the Prodigal can never outrun the Father. That I am not measured by the good I do but by the grace I accept. That being lost is a prerequisite to being found. That living a life of faith is not lived in the light, it is discovered in the dark. That not being a saint here on earth will not necessarily keep you from being in that number when the march begins.

When that march begins, I myself am hoping for a spot in line with the New Orleans cohort, the number that includes a magnificently fully recovered Roman Catholic priest and all the rest too gentle to live among the wolves, the ones who are marching into Zion mostly because we were fortunate enough to stumble into Brennan at the moment when the Word was ready to be spoken into us by one of God's very own.

Thanks be to God for Brennan, and the Truth he has lived, and these pages he has given us.

Robert Benson
The Feast of Saint Mary Magdalene, 2011

To go on the grand tour
A man must be free
From self-necessity.
Patrick Kavanagh, "The Self-Slaved"

A WORD BEFORE

All Is Grace was written in a certain frame of mind—that of a ragamuffin.

Therefore,

This book is by the one who thought he'd
be farther along by now, but he's not.
It is by the inmate who promised the parole
board he'd be good, but he wasn't.
It is by the dim-eyed who showed the path
to others but kept losing his way.
It is by the wet-brained who believed if a
little wine is good for the stomach,
then a lot is great.
It is by the liar, tramp, and thief; otherwise
known as the priest, speaker, and author.
It is by the disciple whose cheese slid
off his cracker so many times
he said "to hell with cheese 'n' crackers."
It is by the young at heart but old
of bone who is led these
days in a way he'd rather not go.

But,

This book is also for the gentle ones
who've lived among wolves.
It is for those who've broken free of collar
to romp in fields of love and marriage and divorce.
It is for those who mourn, who've been
mourning most of their lives,
yet they hang on to *shall be comforted.*
It is for those who've dreamed of entertaining angels
but found instead a few friends of great price.
It is for the younger and elder prodigals
who've come to their senses
again, and again, and again, and again.
It is for those who strain at pious piffle
because they've been swallowed by Mercy itself.
This book is for myself and those who have been around
the block enough times that we dare to whisper
the ragamuffin's rumor—
all is grace.

INTRODUCTION

It's been a while since you've heard from me. Some have wondered if I was even still alive. I am. The last few years of my life have been hard, hard in the sense that things haven't turned out the way I'd planned. In fact, nothing is like I'd planned. I've been uprooted and transplanted in familiar but foreign soil. That sentence is both literal and figurative. I am alive, but it's been hard. I signed the contract to write my memoir almost five years ago now. If I would have sat down right then and there and began writing, this would be a different book. But I didn't.

I delayed writing this book for many reasons, one of them

being that I wrestled with why anyone would want to read a book about my life. I recently asked my friend (and cowriter) John this very question, and his reply was "Brennan, you trust that the crumb of grace will fall." I smiled because that line is from one of my favorite books—*The Diary of a Country Priest*. After more than seventy years of walking on this earth and a good forty of those spent as a vagabond evangelist, I can truly say yes, that is my claim. It's not that I hold that belief so much as that belief holds me.

Saint Paul wrote to the Philippians of "forgetting all that lies behind." A stark literalism here would render memoir a distraction at best. I do not believe that is what Paul intended. My experience has shown me that I all too often tend to deny that which lies behind, but as I still believe, that which is denied cannot be healed.

As Joan Didion once wrote, I want this memoir to put "a narrative line upon disparate images." I've tried to unfold my story as it happened in time, to take you on the grand tour. Some memoirs are prosaic, the root of the word meaning "in a straight line." But my story is less linear, more a circuitous pilgrimage of loops, lapses, hurrahs, and heartaches.

My story is a rosary, the beads of which are the people and experiences that have made me what I am. I have tried to move from one bead to the next, but my fingers are feeble and my eyes are tired. So please forgive me; you will experience gaps and breaks in time and will frequently want to know more. But this is not a tell-all. Sometimes I chose not to elaborate further, and other times I simply cannot remember any more. That's the way it is. But with God's and John's help, this story is as true as I recall.

I have written about experiences with the straight-no-chaser grace of God, battered by wave upon wave of His tender fury. I have also experienced just as many, if not more, moments where Abba's love was mediated, grace via the cloud of witnesses who have cast shadows on my bedraggled, beat-up, and burnt-out life. I have tried to honor those lives in this book. But either way all is well, grace is grace.

The book's subtitle has a qualifier—A *Ragamuffin* Memoir. It's best you know that going in. I fear that word has lost some of its original grit. Ragamuffins have a singular prayer: "God, be merciful to me, a sinner." Any additional flourishes to make that cry more palatable are pharisaical leaven. Warning: Mine has been anything but a straight shot, more like a crooked path filled with thorns and crows and vodka. Prone to wander? You bet. I've been a priest, then an ex-priest. Husband, then ex-husband. Amazed crowds one night and lied to friends the next. Drunk for years, sober for a season, then drunk again. I've been John the beloved, Peter the coward, and Thomas the doubter all before the waitress brought the check. I've shattered every one of the Ten Commandments six times Tuesday. And if you believe that last sentence was for dramatic effect, it wasn't.

Buechner said it best:

> I am inclined to believe that God's chief purpose
> in giving us memory is to enable us to go back in
> time so that if we didn't play those roles right the

first time round, we can still have another go at
it now....

Another way of saying it, perhaps, is that
memory makes it possible for us both to bless the
past, even those parts of it that we have always
felt cursed by, and also to be blessed by it ... what
the forgiveness of sins is all about.[1]

In his essay "Home-Coming," E. B. White recounted a column
written by Bernard DeVoto for *Harper's Magazine*. The columnist
had bemoaned a recent trip to the Maine coast, describing the
highway into Maine as "overpopulated and full of drive-ins, din-
ers, souvenir stands, purulent amusement parks, and cheap-Jack
restaurants." White had recently traveled the same route but
experienced a completely different trip. Sure there were facade-
ridden motor courts next to picturesque clapboard house-barn
combinations and no shortage of opportunities to learn to spell
moccasin while driving in, but there was also more. He saw birch
and spruce and well-proportioned deer and the perfectly designed
fox just there for the asking. But something played a key role in
perception. White concluded,

Probably a man's destination colors the highway, enlarges or diminishes its defects. Gliding over the tar, I was on my way home. DeVoto, traveling the same route, was on his way to what he described rather warily as "professional commitments," by which he probably meant that he was on his way somewhere to make a speech or get a degree. Steering a car toward home is a very different experience from steering a car toward a rostrum, and if our findings differ, it is not that we differed greatly in powers of observation but that we were headed in different emotional directions.[2]

Over the tar of my life, I have usually been headed toward something along the lines of "professional commitments." Or at least I thought they were. But those trips are over now. I am living in a different emotional direction. I am steering toward home, hardly a poster child for anything ... anything, that is, but grace. And what exactly is grace? These pages are my final words on the matter. Grace is everything. I am Brennan the witness.

Tout est Grâce,
Brennan

Part I

RICHARD

I

You don't always get what you ask for. I expect most children have
heard that line in one way or another. It's a difficult lesson to learn,
yet it's one that is essential to growing up. But when I heard my
mother, Amy Manning, say that, I knew she wasn't talking about
something petty like a ball glove or a doll. She was speaking about
something much deeper.

My mother had prayed for a girl. What she got on April 27,
1934, was a boy, me, Richard Manning. My name has not always
been Brennan.

It was the Great Depression in Brooklyn. My brother,

Robert, had been born just fifteen months earlier. Over the years, I've seen many mothers grin and talk about a second child born so quickly on the heels of the first as "my little surprise." But not my mother, not back then. To her, I was one more disappointment, one more unanswered prayer.

My mother was born in Montreal, Canada. At the age of three, both of her parents died within six days of each other in a flu epidemic that swept the city, killing thousands. Those were days when the bedtime prayer "If I should die before I wake" actually had teeth. There was no one to take her in, so my mother was sent to an orphanage. Her stay lasted ten years. God only knows what happened to her in that time. I've wondered if anyone was there to help a three-year-old grieve? Did anyone remember to celebrate her birthday? Did they even know her birthday? What about Christmas—were there gifts for her? Who were the adult females behind those walls and what kinds of mothering impressions, if any, did they make on her? And what about the men? Was my mother abused? Raped? All of this and more are probabilities for that bruised decade of my mother's life. But my questions have no answers because what happened there stayed there. Then again, maybe she would have answered my questions in the same way she answered so many others: *You don't always get what you ask for.*

When she was thirteen, my mother was adopted by a man known as Black George McDonald. Why he adopted her, or any of the details surrounding the adoption, I do not know; I do know that his name sounds like it came straight out of a novel. I've been told that he had made some discoveries of gold and was involved with building the town of Alexandria, between Montreal and Toronto. So Black George evidently had financial means, but I don't know his intentions. He must have had some kindness, however, because my mother wanted to become a nurse and he funded her nursing education. His gift led her to Brooklyn, where she completed her nurse's training, met and married my father, birthed my brother, prayed for a girl, and got me. Although you can clearly deduce that knowing of my mother's disappointment over my birth is painful for me, I have nonetheless committed to try to express gratitude in these pages. So in that spirit, I say, "Thank you, Black George McDonald. I'm not quite sure what all I'm thanking you for, but your grace toward my mother led to my birth, wanted or not. So thanks."

The nurse's training my mother received was based on the popular methods of the 1920s. The word *parenting*, if you can believe it, did not become commonplace until the late 1950s; prior to that it was *childrearing*. The rule was discipline, regimentation, sternness, and a minimum of affection. Early behaviorists like J. B. Watson influenced the thought and approach. Here's a quote that speaks volumes as to the mood of the times: "Mother love is a dangerous instrument that can wreck a child's future chance for happiness." Watson advocated a brisk handshake every morning between parent and child, nothing more. As alien as that sounds now, that was the world into which my brother and I were born. In many ways it was also the world in which my mother grew up.

As I try to understand the mysteries of my life, I must consider the voices and experiences that shaped my mother. Her odyssey from orphan to registered nurse to young mother was nothing less than heroic survival, but heroes don't always make the best parents.

Add to this story a man named Emmett Manning, my father. He and my mother were, in many ways, a pair of contrasts. Unlike my mother, he was not orphaned as a child. In fact, from the time my parents were married, my father's parents lived with us. My mother's father figure was some shadowy benefactor, Black George, but my father's father was a very real alcoholic. I have no idea what my mother lived through as a girl, but I saw glimpses of the rages my father endured as a boy. I learned then that there is more than one way to orphan a child.

Against my mother's nursing degree stood my father's rickety eighth-grade education. Her status as a registered nurse made her quite marketable, even during the Great Depression. She held down two jobs, actually—eight hours a day at St. Mary's Hospital, followed by another shift of private nursing. My father's employment, when it happened, was always described as temporary or part-time.

Temporary and part-time also describe the conversations I recall having with my father. Our words revolved around the subject of correction, *my* correction to be specific. In fact, the word *conversations* is a stretch; they were more like monologues with the same painful ending. I was sent to my room to drop my pants, and my father would whip me with his leather belt. Such displays probably made my father feel a semblance of power, but I knew that even his role as disciplinarian was defined only because my mother, the matriarch, willed it.

Day after day, my father would go out walking, always looking for work, wearing out his shoe leather. But I can't help but believe he was also out looking for something more, something he couldn't have put into words but felt on a daily basis. Maybe he was looking for himself and he knew his father back at the house was no help. Maybe he was looking for dignity, a belief that someone was proud of him. But my mother refused him that kind of respect. I don't know for certain what he searched for, but I do know that every day, he went walking.

You don't always get what you ask for, but you get what you get. Amy was a survivor; Emmett was a searcher. Together they made up the tallest trees in my forest—mother and father.

> *The question that he frames in all but words*
> *Is what to make of a diminished thing.*

Robert Frost, "The Oven Bird"

The cutest baby in Brooklyn

2

That's me at age three. Handsome, huh? My mother entered the snapshot in a contest—"cutest baby in Brooklyn"—or something like that. At the time, I had chubby cheeks, dimples, big blue eyes, and curly golden blond hair. Rationally, I can see that my mother must have felt *some* kind of pride in me or she wouldn't have entered the photo. I ended up winning the contest, but it didn't seem to change the dynamic between my mother and me.

For example, she would often come home in the afternoons between jobs and I would run and throw my arms around her, only to be pushed away. *You're such a nuisance! Go sit in the corner and shut up!* So in one sense, the camera didn't lie; I was a cutie. But in another sense, it did, for in the very next frame I was a nuisance.

That picture came to embody that conflicted sense between my mother and me. During high school, she would pull out the picture and make sure my girlfriends could see how cute I was as a baby. But her pride in that photo never seemed to translate into real life. Children, even eighteen-year-olds, can experience shame, and that's what I felt each time my mother trotted out that picture. I hated it.

Another memory hangs heavy from the December of my sixth year, just a few days before Christmas. My father came home from job hunting to a question he'd heard a hundred times: "Find anything, Emmett?" He gave the all-too-standard answer: "No, Amy. How are the boys?" On this day, my mother pointed to my brother, Rob, and said, "He is born of the Devil, evil, utterly wicked. Emmett, I want you to take him down to the jail right now. Tell the police about him and leave him there."

Now, my brother was seven at the time, hardly old enough to be evil. Still, my father guided Rob's arms into his little navy peacoat and then walked him out the front door and down, I assumed, to the police station. I was scared to death. I scrambled to the windowsill, sat on the ledge, pressed my nose against the frosted glass, and hoped that my father and Rob would turn around and come back inside. I must have sat there for half an hour, waiting, straining to see through my tears and the falling snow. It may have been only fifteen minutes, but terror for a child is measured in breaths, not minutes. Soon, my panic skyrocketed when my father walked back up the street, alone. I was sure in that moment that the next time I disobeyed, I'd be sent to jail for good, just like Rob. But then I saw my brother, trailing a short distance behind my father, kicking at the snow, I imagine my father walked Rob all the way down to the jail, maybe even took him inside to spook him, reprimanded him, then turned and said, "Now let's get home."

I climbed down from the windowsill and assumed the stance common to Rob, my father, and most of the boys I knew—I stood tall because "boys don't cry." But that memory haunted me for over forty dry-eyed years. I still don't know that I've shed tears worthy of the fear I felt that day. Sure I was afraid for myself, but I also didn't know what I would do without Rob.

> *What is my heart to you*
> *That you must break it over and over ...*
> *Practice on something else.*[3]

> Louise Glück, "Matins"

Mom, Dad, me, and Rob

Rob was only a year older than me and in theory could have been an ally in the struggles with our parents. I suppose he also could have sided with them against me. My brother chose neither though; he chose himself. He looked out for one person and one person only—Rob. I don't believe it was selfishness as much as self-preservation. We were still brothers though, both endangered and both trying to find a way to survive what one poet called "the chronic angers of that house."

If I were limited to one word to describe my brother it would be *tough*. But I wouldn't spell it t-o-u-g-h, because that spelling makes me think of d-o-u-g-h, which is soft, and Robert was anything but soft. I like to say that he was t-u-f-f. I can still hear him huff at people or things. It wasn't that he was exasperated; it was more a display of strength and boundaries, like how a bear might paw and snort at the ground. He was very self-possessed, a leader of the kid-gang in the neighborhood who loved to fight and didn't appear to need a drop of affection from my mother. Tuff. As younger brothers often do, I loved him and loathed him equally.

Rob and I used to play a game called Clock with the neighborhood kids. Today it would be considered silly, if not outright stupid. But it was a different time then. Here's how the game worked: A group of kids, maybe five or six, would sit on a bench or stoop, and the game leader, who always had a watch, would ask, "What time is it?" The object was to guess the correct time. An incorrect guess and you were eliminated from the game. Eventually someone would guess the time, earning the right to be the leader for the next round. Somehow we could repeat that same game numerous times every day.

One day we were playing Clock and I was the leader. Earlier that day Rob had been especially mean to me, chasing me around the dining-room table with a butcher knife, pretending to be a villain or something. I knew he only meant to spook me, but he had succeeded a little too well that morning. So I decided to get back at him. My brother may have been tuff, but I could be shrewd.

That particular day we were playing Clock just outside our front door, which was usually locked. However, with a fine scheme in mind, I had left it unlocked. I went down the row of kids asking, "What time is it?" I finally came to Rob. When he gave the wrong answer, I hit him as hard as I could across the face. I immediately turned and bolted through the front door, locking it behind me. He was left banging on the door, screaming, "I'm gonna kill him!" I can only imagine the stunned looks on the other kids' faces.

Obviously Rob didn't kill me, and as time eased on the literal clock, so did his anger. But I gained a little status that day in the eyes of our peers. My brother was the toughest kid in the neighborhood and no one had ever dared to hit him. But I did and lived to tell about it. I never asked Rob about it, but I believe he was proud of me that day. That's what I meant when I said I didn't know what I would have done if my brother had been left in jail that day. Our brother-to-brother relationship was often antagonistic, but he was still a witness that I had some grit about me. I needed that presence because some days I thought I might disappear.

3

My memories of my father's father, William Manning, are shy at best. I avoided him as much as I could. He had a work-related injury that prevented him from holding down a regular job. Most of what he held down was alcohol. I have no recollection of him being mean to me, no abuse or anything like that. I was there when he would try to rage at my grandmother or my father, but by that time he was more like a toothless shark. My guess is that was not the case when my father was a boy.

What I did like about my grandfather was that he was married to my grandmother. Anna Manning was a stereotypical

Irishwoman minus the temper. I loved her. She was beautiful. She stood maybe five-foot-three, but what she lacked in stature she more than made up for in her kind face crowned with snow white hair. The renowned psychologist Alice Miller introduced the concept of the "enlightened witness"—somebody both able and willing to take a child's side and protect him or her from any dangers of abuse. My grandmother was my enlightened witness. With her in our house, I felt safe. I felt loved and accepted too, but primarily safe. I do not remember her ever saying an unkind word to or about my mother. She appeared to understand the tenuous state of our household, and she respected its design. However, that did not mean she would stand by silently and watch me be mistreated. She was skilled in the art of disarmament—the craft of using a word or tone to diffuse my mother's anger. I've often thought that she learned that art by living with an alcoholic husband, learning what to say and what not to say, and when to speak and when not to speak. Then again, my grandmother may have come by the gift naturally; perhaps God knew she would need that skill in this life, so He gave it to her in spades. However she came by it, I'm just glad she did.

Of all my books, *The Boy Who Cried Abba* is one of my personal favorites. It tells the story of Willie Juan, a somewhat autobiographical character. One of the main characters is Willie Juan's grandmother. Her character had lived a very different life in her youth; she spent time looking for love and happiness in the wrong places. But then a great change occurred, and she gave up her old ways of living and changed her name to Calm Sunset. Here is an excerpt describing her tenderness toward her grandson, who had just been bullied: "My sweet Willie Juan, the way you were treated today is not a new thing.... People often think ... they can be mean to you because no one will step forward to protect you." Calm Sunset was very much based on my grandmother. Calm Sunset stepped forward for Willie Juan, as my grandmother did for me. My mother was right—you don't always get what you ask for. But early on I questioned whether she was only half right. I sorta believed sometimes you get so much more.

In the darkest days of the Great Depression people talked of the "big bad wolf" and "the wolf always being at the door." That image reflected the pervasive fear felt in all our lives in such hard times. In fact the song "Who's Afraid of the Big Bad Wolf?" became an anthem of those days, an attempt to encourage everyone to hold our chins up. But another image back then trumped the wolf for me, what I've since heard described as the "invisible dragon." This monster wasn't at the door and big and bad; it was inside, subtle and devouring. Shame.

As I think back on my childhood, the word *shame* serves as an umbrella. It is the sense of being completely insufficient as a person, the nagging feeling that for some reason you're defective and unworthy. That's how I felt all the time. And just as there is only one word to describe it, one experience in my memory has a similar kind of all-encompassing sweep, a moment in time that gave shape to my entire world. I hinted about this experience in my book *Abba's Child*, but I want to give it a deeper telling here. Why? Well, now I'm not so afraid of dragons.

The memory came back to me one day while I was on a long retreat in the Colorado Rockies, a much-needed stint of therapy and solitude. I spent my mornings under the caring hand of a psychologist who helped me revisit memories of my childhood. One crisp morning as I talked with the psychologist, I became startled by the realization that there was an absolute void of feeling in my life. It was like I could not access anything emotionally. I realized that I hadn't felt anything for a long, long time, since I was about eight years old. In working with the psychologist, I remembered something that happened back then, something sinister that had irreparably darkened my life.

My mother had come home one afternoon from a shift of nursing. For some reason I greeted her harshly, saying, "You love Robert more than me, don't you? You've always loved him more! I hate you!"

My mother looked stunned, but I didn't relent. I continued to accuse her. "The truth is Robert's always been your favorite. You've always been kind to him and mean to me!"

She grew angry. "Stop that! Stop saying that. You stop that now!"

My mother then stormed toward me and began punching me, over and over, to the point where I fell on the floor. She straddled me and continued to punch me, screaming, "Shut up! Shut up!"

My grandmother then entered the room, and her calm voice halted things. "Amy, you better stop. You're going to hurt him." This is what I meant about disarming: She didn't come in shouting at my mother, as one would imagine she would do. She was calm and somehow knew that her gentle approach would make my mother stop.

Whether it was immediate or gradual, I don't remember. All I know is that the punching stopped. There had been occasions before that moment when I questioned my value as a person, but that experience, when I was eight years old, confirmed my unworthiness. I felt like I would disappear into a pile of ashes.

Shame—what happened when my mother, the dragon, huffed and puffed and blew my self down.

Under my psychologist's care, I realized that after that event, I had placed a muzzle on my emotional self. I had no feeling, no nothing. I had vowed it.

For days, I sat with that memory in the beauty of Colorado, trying to refeel it and grieve it as best I could. After taking some time to process that memory, my therapist then encouraged me to take a further step and not to think of my mother as the dragon. What my hard inner work those days exposed was a shame-bound family, a group of people, all crammed into a small space, each feeling uniquely alone, a cast of characters loyal to a pattern that promoted secrets and inhibited intimate relationships. Mine was a childhood of repeated rejection and punishment or the threat of it.

My grandmother Anna Manning and me

And as I've grown to believe, so was the childhood of my parents and probably their parents. As my friend Richard Rohr said, "If we don't learn to transform the pain, we'll transfer it." I realized my mother wasn't the dragon; she was another victim of the dragon. But the dragon doesn't die easily, so the shame just kept passing down the generations. I fear I've passed it along as well.

Vow. It's an old-fashioned word, usually heard only around weddings and even then not so much anymore. I made a vow with myself following my mother's cruelty: I would become a good boy. These words from Alice Miller explain it perfectly:

> Children who fulfill their parents' conscious or unconscious wishes are "good," but if they ever refuse to do so or express wishes of their own that go against those of their parents, they are called egoistic and inconsiderate.... If a child brought up this way does not wish to lose his parents' love (And what child can risk that?), he must learn very early to share, to give, to make sacrifices, and to be willing to "do without."[4]

So I decided, at the ripe old age of eight, to accommodate and do whatever it took to ensure approval, especially my mother's. I would not talk back, not ask questions, and be seen but not heard.

What I had no way of realizing at the time is that there is a fine line between vows and deals, and deals can be sneaky, under-the-table things. At the very least, the deals I made with myself to be a "good boy" cost me my voice, my sense of wonder, and my self-worth for most of my adult life. The invisible dragon roared, I cowered, and what I call the "impostor" was born, a shadow to my eight-year-old life. The impostor is a fake version of yourself, and that's exactly how I started living. I faked being happy when I was sad, I faked being excited when I was disappointed, I even faked being nice when inside I was really angry. I still looked and sounded like me, but I wasn't me. I was a fake. I lived as an impostor of myself. But living as the impostor will do nothing but harm. Here's a quick list of how the impostor functions, bullet-pointed because it can just about kill you:

- The impostor lives in fear.
- The impostor is consumed with a need for acceptance and approval.
- The impostor is codependent; in other words, out of touch with his or her own feelings.
- The impostor's life is a herky-jerky existence of elation and depression. The impostor is what he or she does.
- The impostor demands to be noticed.

- The impostor cannot experience intimacy in any relationship.
- And last but not least, the impostor is a liar.

Shakespeare described love as an "ever-fixed mark." In a healthy family, you know how love is defined: It's clear, has boundaries, and is attainable. Unfortunately, in a shame-bound family, love is a moving target; one day it's this and one day it's that, and just when you're sure you've got it figured out, you discover you don't.

One Christmas—I must have been ten years old—I spent some time walking the creaky wooden floors of Woolworth's five-and-dime searching for a gift for my mother. I happened upon a little notepad, the kind people used to keep beside telephones. It was multicolored, pastels of pink and green and blue. I'd never seen anything like it. I thought it was gorgeous, surely something that would thrill my mother. Christmas morning came, and we were all there—my parents and grandparents, my brother and sister and me. As my mother began opening my gift, I held my breath in anticipation. She tore the wrapping paper away and just stared at the notepad. "What in God's name am I gonna do with this? What a waste of money!" After what felt like an eternity where all eyes in the room were on me, my mother tossed me the pad, and the Mannings moved on to other gifts. I felt like I'd purchased the Hope Diamond for her, but it wasn't enough. I just didn't understand. I was crushed.

4

I mentioned my sister, Geraldine, but I haven't really introduced her. Like I said earlier, my mother had prayed for a girl.
I never heard her say that out loud or anything, but believe
me, I knew. Her prayers were finally answered in 1943 with the
birth of my sister. I was nine years old, and I remember that
Gerry's arrival brought a change to our household. Things were
a little sweeter. I can't say exactly how they were sweeter, they
just were. For example, I remember watching my mother fix
Gerry's hair in the evenings, sometimes taking half an hour to
get it just right.

Looking back, maybe it wasn't so much that my mother or father had become sweeter. Maybe it was just that Gerry's own innate sweetness had a ripple effect.

After my sister's birth, my mother continued working during the daytime while my father kept looking for work and my brother roamed on his own. That left me to be my sister's keeper.

Many mornings I would take Gerry by the hand and walk her up to McKinley Park in Brooklyn. We'd play there until my mother or father came home in the afternoon. I would always pack us a lunch of peanut butter and jelly sandwiches and a Coke. We loved to swing and slide and seesaw, but our favorite spot was the sandbox. I can't speak for my sister, but for me the sandbox was a place of pure play—of childlikeness. It had definite boundaries, but inside those edges I was free to build and dig and just be. The "being" part was something I had lost; it was never allowed at home. I wish it would have been, but it wasn't. So trips to the park to babysit were not a chore for me, a boy of twelve. They were a sanctuary.

Betty Smith published *A Tree Grows in Brooklyn* in 1943, the year of my sister's birth. The book tells the story of dreamer Francie Nolan and her younger beloved brother, Neeley. Surrounding the lives of the children are Katie, the hardworking, breadwinning mother, and Johnny, the often-unemployed alcoholic father. Sounds sorta familiar, doesn't it? Although my sister and I are quite different, I believe we both shared hopes like Francie's:

My sister, Geraldine, and me

Let me be *something* every minute of every hour
of my life. Let me be gay; let me be sad. Let me
be cold; let me be warm. Let me be hungry ...
have too much to eat. Let me be ragged or well
dressed. Let me be sincere—be deceitful. Let me
be truthful; let me be a liar. Let me be honorable
and let me sin. Only let me be *something* every
blessed minute. And when I sleep, let me dream
all the time so that not one little piece of living
is ever lost.[5]

The "tree" in the novel is called *ailanthus altissima*, or the
Tree of Heaven. It's a pivotal metaphor used to represent the ability
to thrive in a harsh setting. Here is Smith's description:

Some people called it the Tree of Heaven. No
matter where its seed fell, it made a tree which
struggled to reach the sky. It grew in boarded-up
lots and out of neglected rubbish heaps and it was
the only tree that grew out of cement. It grew
lushly but only in the tenements districts.[6]

It's strange because there I was—in my opinion this worth-
less thing in my mother's eyes—charged with responsibility for

my sister: "You keep an eye out for her now," my mother said. I felt like one of those Trees of Heaven, growing up in a severe environment, reaching and struggling. I like to think that maybe my branches provided a shade for Gerry in those days, a person she could look up to and feel safe with. I believed she loved me then, as I believe she loves me now. I wouldn't say either one of us necessarily grew "lushly," but we did grow.

Once, I remember my mother talking to my father about me. She said, "Richard's just a dreamer, Emmett. That's why he'll never amount to much."

In a way, she was right. I was a dreamer, and still am. Some people have recurring nightmares, ones that chase them for seasons or possibly for life. As a boy, I had a recurring daydream, not one of horror but of hope. In the dream, a boy my age approached me and said, "I like you. Can we play together?"

Playing—whether with my sister or with the boys in my neighborhood—was a great escape for me. I mentioned that the neighborhood boys and I used to play Clock. It was a fun game, but as we grew older, as you can imagine, the thrill seemed to fade. Stickball was for the older boys; you had to be at least twelve to play. Ringolevio, however, was a game for every kid. It's basically a combination of tag and hide-and-seek. There are two teams, the pursued and the pursuers. One team goes off to hide and the other team goes looking for them. If a pursuer finds and catches you, then you have to go sit on the stoop in front of someone's house; we called it "jail." One day's game was particularly memorable.

I thought I'd found a great hiding spot, one nobody could find. But then all of a sudden Joey was there. As I just typed that name—Joey—I felt an ache behind my breastbone. His arrival proved to be life changing.

Joey Keegan lived down the street and had brown-blond hair and Irish blue eyes. I had seen him before, but I don't think we had ever talked. But that day Joey found me and instead of sending me to jail, he said, "I like you. Can we play together?" Yes, that's right, the very words from my dream.

It's hard for me to express how thrilling it was to hear those words. They were a compliment, and in our family, direct compliments were rare; they presumably contributed to the sin of pride, the kind that usually comes before a great fall.

After our game that day, I found myself rehearsing those words from Joey, trying to convince myself I hadn't made them up. But sure enough, in the days and weeks that followed, Joey would repeat them, out loud, as we'd play together—"I like playing with you." Joey Keegan had become my first best friend, and I have good cause to believe I was his.

Joey and I were typical boys. One afternoon, for example, I asked him if he could change his name to any name in the world, what would it be. He said, "Ludwig Niemanschnifter." I thought that was so funny; we both died laughing. When I asked where that name came from, Joey just said, "I like the sound of it." As you could probably guess, Joey turned the question on me. To this day I don't know where this came from, but I blurted out, "Otsio Motsio Zine Ferein." We both died laughing again. My friendship with Joey—or "Ludwig" as I called him after that—was a dream come true, but unfortunately the dream didn't last long.

I never remember thinking that Joey might have been sick. I don't recall his parents or mine ever saying anything about it. Maybe I was so taken with the dream that I missed what would have been obvious to someone else. I don't know. What I do know is that one day an ambulance showed up in front of his house and took him to the hospital. The next day I got ready to rush to his house to play tag or throw the Spalding ball against the bricks. My father was home that day. He stopped me and said, "You can't go to Joey Keegan's anymore, Richard." The three-letter question of childhood then dropped from my lips—"Why?" My father took a deep breath and then told me, "Because he died last night."

I was later told that Joey had a brain tumor, although I really didn't know what that meant.

That experience was my introduction to death. I'd seen dead birds before and even a dead cat, but never a person, never someone close to me. Everyone I knew was healthy; certainly no one had brain tumors. My parents didn't know Joey's family that well, but they came with me to the funeral out of respect. As we filed by the casket, I remember feeling terribly lost again. Without Joey, there wouldn't be anyone to come find me.

My brother, Rob, always ran in a pack, but that never

appealed to me. I always wanted just one friend, someone like Joey. I did have a few Joey-like friends after that: Bill Hennison, Frankie Farley, and Harry Wiley. In fact, Harry and I went to game six of the 1947 World Series between the Yankees and the Dodgers. We got up at 1:00 a.m. and waited until the gates opened at 10:00 a.m. We were among the last ones to get tickets before they sold out. That was quite a game and quite a memory. But even so, there was nobody like Joey. He was the one who had said the words from my dream—"I like you. Can we play together?" He had voiced the deep desire I felt, something I had asked for. But like my mother said, you don't always get what you ask for. Or maybe if you do, it doesn't last long.

Joey's death occurred alongside an argument my mother was having with our landlord. He was raising our rent, and my mother was furious; she thought it was illegal. So she began planning our move. Not that there would have been much anyway, but any talk of Joey's death took a backseat in our family to the panic of our raised rent. So I experienced the death of a friend in conjunction with being uprooted to a new place. We moved quickly, blocks away to a whole new neighborhood, new school, new kids.

Joey's death took me by surprise and forced me to grow up fast. I realized that not only was my household this fragile place where anything could happen, but other kids' homes were too. Another experience with death revealed that even the whole world was dangerous.

I vividly recall the day in December 1941 when my father called me into the living room. We had one of those great big radios. He said, "Just be quiet and listen." The next voice I heard was President Franklin Delano Roosevelt's: "Yesterday, December 7, 1941—a date which will live in infamy …" There was such gravity to his voice as he talked about Pearl Harbor, and I felt sad for all those killed the day before. I didn't know any of their names, but the president made it all feel so personal. But whereas Joey's death was marked only by sadness, that day was also marked with pride. The president challenged we the people to sacrifice, to make something good out of something bad. That kind of hope was absent from Joey's death; it was just a wound. But as strange as it might sound, December 7, 1941, was a wound filled with hope. It is the day I remember feeling like I'd become a man.

5

It could be said that my parents were many things, but two of the many were for certain—Irish and Roman Catholic. They wanted their children to continue that heritage too, so the grade schools I attended were etched with names like St. Anselm's and Our Lady of Angels. The education I received was comparable to that of most schools; however, Our Lady of Angels was considered the premier grammar school in all of Brooklyn. The fact that my mother made sure I attended a prestigious school might seem to contradict my feelings of unworthiness. But it doesn't. For the shame-bound family, appearances are everything, and my mother made sure that on the outside we looked respectable, as if we fit in with the Irish-Catholics around us.

The heart of the pedagogy in those schools was *repetitio est mater studiorum*—"repetition is the mother of study." The Ten Commandments are forever tucked inside my brain alongside "thirty days hath September, April, June, and November," complemented by the multiplication and division tables. The instruction in our classrooms came from nuns, also known as sisters. I don't remember any of them looking much like Julie Andrews, but some possessed a different kind of beauty.

One such lady was Sister Thomasina. I bet other students believed they were her favorite, but I would argue that I was the one. At least that was the feeling she conveyed to me each day. She was one of those women who never seemed to have a bad day; I'm sure she did, but I guess I missed them. She was motherly to me, a warm feminine figure in contrast to my mother's cold edge. Sister Thomasina's gift was encouragement, and she frequently told me how bright I was and how well I was doing in school. The encouragement was verbal, but it was also transferred directly into my bones via a hand on my shoulder and her radiant smile. Sure, I had a schoolboy's crush on her.

I grew to love reading and writing—they came naturally to me, and they are two love affairs I've faithfully kept throughout my life. I guess my first inkling of possibly becoming a writer was probably because of an assignment from my English teacher, Sister Mary Frances. The assignment was simple enough: Write a paragraph about something that happened in your family the day before. My single paragraph quickly grew to six pages. The gist of the story was a jog I took, and along the way I tripped and fell down. I wrote, "All of a sudden I realized I was in soft cement and I couldn't get out." My brother, Rob, was playing nearby and heard my cry for help. He came over and hauled me out.

The rest of the story is that by the time I got home, the cement had begun to harden on my pants. My mother was furious that she was going to have to buy me another pair; my safety seemed only an afterthought. I knew that if my mother saw her fury in print, she'd have my father punish me. Remember, appearances were everything. So in one of my first self-edits I ended the story with being rescued by my brother. Sister Mary Frances returned my story with an A across the top. She had made only one correction, changing "all of a sudden" to "suddenly." Her gentle corrective surprised me; it was so different from what I experienced at home. All of a sudden I felt that someone believed in me. Or I should say "suddenly."

Reading and writing I enjoyed, but religion not so much. When I was a boy, God was a stained-glass ceiling, a deity way up and out there, remote, big, and harsh. There is a descriptive phrase I've used for my early view of God, taken from Flannery O'Connor's "Turkey" story: God was the "Something Awful." Flannery wrote of her protagonist, Ruller: "He ran faster and faster, and as he turned up the road to his house, his heart was running as fast as his legs and he was certain that Something Awful was tearing behind him with its arms rigid and its fingers ready to clutch."[7] That's how I felt about God in those Catholic grade-school years. I never heard any reference to a loving, personal God. The emphasis was on obeying the Ten Commandments in order to avoid punishment.

In that sense, the religious aspect of school was similar to home. In addition to believing God was "something awful," I also experienced Him as "separate." A good way to try to explain this is to describe my experience in the confessional booth. One of the priests sat on his side and I sat on mine. I couldn't see the priest, but at the right time I could hear him. Every once in a while the priest would be gentle, and our conversation would go something like this:

> Me: Bless me, Father, for I have sinned. It has been a week since my last confession. I hit my brother. I spit at my brother. And I have disobeyed my parents.
> Priest: That was a very good confession. You prepared it well. And you have my blessing.... For your penance say three "Our Fathers" and three "Hail Marys."

But most of the time I swear it seemed like the priest was angry. He was often almost screaming, something like this:

> Priest: Don't you have any respect for your parents? How dare you disobey them! Tell me exactly what you did and do not leave anything out!
> Me: My mother sent me to the store to buy a pound of lean bacon and I forgot and bought a pound of fatty. My mother got angry because I disobeyed.

Through the voices of those angry priests, I heard an awful, angry God separate from me and my life. So, like I did at home, I vowed to do what was required for me to avoid punishment: I tried my best to be a good Catholic boy. I even mustered up the courage and tried out one year to be an altar boy, but for some reason I couldn't memorize the Latin. I knew that I had disappointed the priest (he told me as much), which meant I obviously had disappointed God (why would God disagree with the priest?), and that reinforced my mother's words about me (which she'd said more than once): *He'll never amount to much.*

As wonderful as the encouragements were from those like Sister Thomasina and Sister Mary Frances, they paled in comparison to my mother's dismissive voice in my head—*just a dreamer.* I don't like the word *just.*

There is a scene in the movie *Finding Neverland* where young Peter Davies is describing Porthos, J. M. Barrie's dog.

> Peter: This is absurd. It's just a dog.
> Barrie: Just a dog? Just?
> [to Porthos] Porthos, don't listen.
> [to Peter] Porthos dreams of being a bear, and you want to shatter those dreams by saying he's just a dog? What a horrible candle-snuffing word. That's like saying, "He can't climb that mountain, he's just a man," or, "That's not a diamond, it's just a rock."[8]

So to appease God and the priests and my parents, I went

to Mass on Sundays. But any prayers I might have had, I kept to
myself. I didn't want to be a bear; I just wanted to be me, although
I wasn't quite sure who that was.

I wish I could share more specific memories like this from
my early childhood, but I can't. I wish I could remember more
words and phrases spoken by my parents or friends or teachers, but
I can't. As I said, the decision to become a good boy effectively cut
me off at the roots and that probably stunted my memory as well.
I guess a good way to summarize my life from age six to sixteen was
that it was a decade of doing what I could to be a good, obedient
boy. I'm not particularly proud of that summary, that's just the way
it was. But things would change.

6

At the age of sixteen, Sunday mornings still looked the same. I still showed up at Sunday-morning Mass and experienced the same distant God. But something different began on Saturday nights. I started drinking.

If someone had shown me a genogram filled with circles and squares denoting the sap of alcohol in my family's tree, I might have seen it coming. My father had struggled with it, his father had struggled with it, and who knows about the men before them. But no such graphs were around, and my father and grandfather weren't talking about it, and I'm pretty sure I wasn't interested in listening to them at age sixteen anyway. I was young and horribly insecure and willing to try anything to not feel that way. You should know, however, that from this point on, you'd be wise to consider anything I say about alcohol to be suspect. It's not that what I'm saying isn't true; it's that what I'm saying only scratches the surface.

As I said, I was sixteen. I was working as a delivery boy for one of the local grocery stores, getting paid on Saturdays. Every Saturday night I slipped into a pattern I would follow for years: Get paid and go drink draft beers, one after the other. I don't remember my first drink or anything like that; it wasn't a profound moment. I almost wish I could remember it so that I could share the blame with someone or something. What I do remember was the result, the buzz. Drinking gave me a rush of confidence, and for a boy hounded by feelings of inadequacy, the buzz was a welcome relief. What was impossible to realize at the time was that I was shooting myself in the head in some strange time warp where the bullet takes many years to finally reach its target.

At age eighteen I experienced my first alcohol-induced blackout at the hand of Seagram's. Usually the absolute terror of blacking out stops people in their tracks. As one boozer said, "The feathers on your chin mean you ate the parakeet." But it didn't stop me. By the age of twenty I had acquired the nickname Funnel, no doubt because I drank a dozen or so beers every night, five days a week, a pint of rye whiskey every other day, and often a liter of sake once a week. Those were days of sheer volume. My threshold was such that I endured hangovers and still functioned well in most situations, or as someone dear to me once said, "You can go to town and still hold court."

I don't ever remember getting caught by my parents. If I was sixteen, that would make my sister seven, and my mother's focus was on Gerry, as it should have been. I'm willing to bet my mother had some idea, seeing as how my father struggled with alcohol too. But maybe at that age she thought I was going to do what I was going to do. As for my father, I believe he knew as well but perhaps felt he had waited too long to broach the topic with me. If some things aren't said before a boy leaves home, it's probably too late. I do wish my father might have tried to say something, anything. But I don't believe he got those kinds of fathering "cards" from his father, and as my mother said, "If you don't get 'em, you can't play 'em."

7

My decision to attend college was mainly fueled by encouragements concerning my writing I had received along the way. I
enrolled in St. John's University in Queens with an eye toward
being a sportswriter. I remember two things about my freshman
year at St. John's: that I had a gift and that I liked to drink.

I learned about the gift in a speech class I was taking. I
can't remember the content of the speech I gave in class that day,
but the class response was positive. My professor asked to see me
briefly after class. He didn't prolong the moment but simply said,
"Richard, you've been given a great gift. Use it well." That was

the very first time anyone had said anything about my ability to speak, probably because that was one of my first public-speaking experiences. I'm hesitant to say my professor's words changed everything, but they did change something, something about how I saw myself. Sometimes one sentence can stand up against years of hearing "He won't amount to much." I was thrilled my professor believed in me, but I was also just a little unnerved. Someone had given me a "great gift," which meant that somebody beyond my professors believed in me, maybe somebody big.

The other memory of my freshman year is just as vivid but not nearly so poignant. By some miracle I was a B student, even though I don't remember ever studying. What I do remember is drinking. Larry Chaffee and I would go down to the Dodger Cafe after classes, about 2:30 p.m., and drink until dusk. Some days I would skip class, but I had perfect attendance at the Dodger Cafe; everyone there knew my name.

Early in my sophomore year at St. John's three of my friends—Joe Mulligan, Tom Fitzgerald, and Charlie Peterson— decided to join the Marines. They threw the invitation my way to join them, and I said, "Sure, why not?" I don't think I joined because of peer pressure but more because of the feeling of potential it gave me. I remember thinking that I could either stay in college, or I could join the Marines and I might just win the Silver Star, possibly nab a Purple Heart, maybe even a Bronze Star, potentially come home to a hero's welcome. Then those closest to me would finally approve of and affirm me. So in the spur-of-the-moment way college sophomores often behave, I dropped out of St. John's in October 1952, and as an eighteen-year-old, I enlisted in the Marine Corps.

Sooner than I expected, I had moved to Parris Island, South Carolina, for basic training. On my first day, I was among forty other young men getting cleaned up and then experiencing esprit de corps by having our heads shaved.

Drill instructors are notorious for being able to spot hopers and dreamers like me, and Sergeant James Whistler put a bead on me from the very beginning. One morning he approached me and asked, "Did you shave this morning, boy?" I lied through my teeth and said yes; the most I had grown at the time was peach fuzz. But the Sergeant liked clean and smooth. He retreated on a dime and returned with a dry razor and the command to "Shave! Now!" I was trying to be a good Marine, so I stood in formation and shaved. Although shaving cream or lotion would have been nice, I would have easily settled for some water, but I had nothing but the razor. I nicked myself so many times it wasn't funny; there was blood all over the razor. That was a pretty good introduction to the Marine's strong belief in the chain of command and the gung-ho attitude that followed.

Following the weeks of basic training, my friend Joe Mulligan and I were assigned to the Ammunition Demolition School in Quantico, Virginia. We worked with every kind of weapon the corps had at the time, learning the intricacies of everything from rifles to howitzers. The feeling was strong among us that deployment to Korea was not if, but when. Saturday nights found the

Back: Tom Fitzgerald, Charlie Peterson
Front: me, Joe Mulligan

enlisted men at the beer hall trying to forget about life for a while. I had no problem with that. One Saturday night about midnight we were sitting around drinking beer and I offered to get one last pitcher. A man by the name of Ray Brennan had joined us a few minutes earlier and said, "None for me, thanks." I couldn't believe it—"What? What's the matter with you?" He turned to me and said, "I'm meetin' the rail tomorrow."

What Ray meant was going to Communion. The rule in the Catholic Church was nothing to eat or drink after midnight if you were planning to receive Holy Communion the next morning. Now here's a strange thing. While those words "meetin' the rail tomorrow" registered with me, I also heard something entirely different: "I'd like to be your friend." Don't ask me how I heard it that way, but I did. It must have been something in the look on his face or the tone of his voice. So I got another pitcher and drank while Ray sat and refrained, and in the days that followed, we forged a friendship that outlasted our time in the Marines.

We were given a ten-day leave prior to heading to Korea. I invited Ray to Brooklyn and he agreed with the proviso that we'd stop in Chicago to see his parents as well. I thought it was a swell idea. Ray introduced me to his family as "my best friend."

It was then that I met Frances Brennan, Ray's mom. She and I had a great connection, and from that point on, that lady doted on me as if I were her own. And in many ways after that day, I was.

We left for Brooklyn, and I introduced Ray to my family in the same way, as "my best friend." My family was cordial enough to Ray, but the atmosphere was full of fear; you see, in a few days we were headed to LaGuardia Airport to depart for Korea. My brother had shipped off to Korea about a year earlier, so here I was, the next son, going in to harm's way as well. It was strange in a way, knowing that could be the last time I would see my family. I don't think any of us quite knew how to feel. My family did know what to do though: They came to the airport to see us off. In a move that caught me off guard, my father stepped forward, shook my hand, and said, "Good luck, son. Come back safe." I felt closer to my father on that day than I had in years, maybe ever. Ray and I left for Korea, arriving there in June 1953. One month later the armistice was signed, and the war was over. All my thoughts of potentially coming home a war hero dissolved. *If you don't get the cards, you can't play 'em.*

What remained was a three-year commitment to the few and the proud as an ammunition demolition expert. I don't remember all the details of what happened next, but our division was sent to Japan for eighteen months. During that time I decided to play the hand I'd been dealt and use the time to work on something I enjoyed—my writing.

I adored the sportswriter Red Smith, and I read and studied all the columns he wrote. He was the first writer I ever tried to copy stylewise. Our Marine division put out a weekly newspaper, and I started sending in comments on some of the articles, especially the ones that had anything to do with sports. Someone must have taken notice, because the next thing I knew, I had my military occupation specialty switched from ammunition demolition expert to combat correspondent. I was transferred to a newspaper office where I was given writing assignments, some of which involved covering sporting events. Whatever strange disappointment I felt that the war had ended was soon eclipsed by the opportunity to do something I loved and receive positive affirmation for it. George Wilson, a technical sergeant in charge of the newspaper, told me more than once, "You know, you're a good writer."

8

As a member of the armed services, I could apply for tuition assistance to pursue an undergraduate or graduate degree from a college or university. After going through a ton of red tape, I received an early discharge in 1955 and began the fall semester at the University of Missouri, determined to pursue my dream of becoming a writer. At that time the University of Missouri had one of the premier programs in journalism. I had no idea I was about to have a dream within a dream. I've recounted this experience in my books and talks over the years. I repeat it here because of its profound importance in my life.

I was roused one morning from a startling dream. The dream was essentially that I had achieved all my aspirations of status and station. You might call it "the pretty dream"—pretty wife, pretty exclusive home, pretty fast car, pretty great money, and pretty impressive literary awards like the Nobel Prize for Literature. I woke up in horror to exclaim, "My God, there's got to be more!" For a twenty-one-year-old about to set sail on a course for "pretty," the dream was nothing short of troubling. I thought I'd finally found some direction and purpose, a path to be me. But that dream stopped everything in its tracks when I felt that having it all wouldn't be enough. It's hard to know too much when you're in your early twenties, but I did know that I didn't want to live the rest of my life only to be, as Goethe put it, "a troubled guest on the dark earth."

There's no way I would have described myself at that age as religious, much less spiritual, but nevertheless I made an appointment to visit the spiritual director on campus. I needed someone to talk to, someone to try to help me interpret my dream. I would so like to honor that man's name in print; I do wish I could remember his name, but I can't. He listened intently to my description of the dream, followed by my troubled plea for "more." That gentle man looked at me and said, "Richard, maybe the 'more' is God."

A casual observer might look at my decision to join the Marines as one made on a whim; my friends and I just decided to do it. There's some truth to that. The same observer might look at my decision to leave the University of Missouri after only one semester and enter a Franciscan seminary as equally whimsical, maybe even foolhardy. But I would resist that. No friends accompanied me in that departure; in fact, I had little, if any, support. And while the military decision held the possibility of fame, that spiritual decision had the potential for "more." More what? I wasn't exactly sure, but like the disciples who dropped their nets and followed Jesus, I dropped my well-laid plans and followed my new dream.

I've written before that this was when I embarked on my search for God. But I'm really not certain I could have articulated what I was actually searching for; words like *meaning* and *purpose* held just as much weight for me as *God*. It was definitely a confusing time made even more difficult by my family's inability to extend mercy or wisdom. I believe they saw my decision to enter the Franciscan seminary in Loretto, Pennsylvania, as nothing more than an epic display of cowardice. My brother, Rob, even bet me fifty dollars I wouldn't last a week in the seminary. To them, I was like Joseph Conrad's Lord Jim. Conrad wrote it perfectly:

> It is when we try to grapple with another man's intimate need that we perceive how incomprehensible, wavering, and misty are the beings that share with us the sight of the stars and the warmth of the sun.[9]

I did last a week at seminary, but barely. Looking back, going from a uniformed Marine to a robed brother may not have been the smartest next step in my quest for "more." I admit it was a rather dramatic move, one I was not prepared for.

After a week in Loretto, I packed my bags. I decided that I had given God a sporting chance. I hadn't lost all sense of decorum though, so I felt it appropriate to tell Father Augustine "So long." I stopped by his office on my way out, but he wasn't in. It was nearly noon.

It's been said that "we cannot kill time without injuring eternity." I'm not sure that's true, because in an effort to kill time waiting for Father Augustine's return, I visited the chapel, and in my case, eternity was forever altered. I decided to grab a prayer book and visit the fourteen stations of the cross. Stations 1–11 remain a blur; maybe they were a necessary prelude, something to get me warmed up.

The word *synesthesia* describes what happened to me at station 12. Synesthesia is a union of the senses, one type of stimulation evoking the sensation of another. Station 12 is "Jesus dies on the cross." I was instructed to kneel, so I did. I remember feeling the solidity of the floor. Then the Angelus bell from a nearby monastery gave its noontime toll in the distance. And then I read these words on the page:

> Behold Jesus crucified! Behold His wounds, received for love of you! His whole appearance betokens love: His head is bent to kiss you; His arms are extended to embrace you; His heart is

open to receive you. O superabundance of love,
Jesus, the Son of God, dies upon the cross, that
man may live and be delivered from everlasting
death!

The next thing I knew, it was a few minutes after three
o'clock in the afternoon. Just what happened in those three hours?
I was a Marine after all, and soldiers don't just lose three hours. But
I did; all I know is that I had been in another, magnificent realm.
The religious scholar Mircea Eliade has referred to this realm as the
"Golden World." I could not agree more.

For three hours I found myself in *terra incognita*. It was the
very heart of Jesus Christ, the place of unconditional love. To have
experienced just the terrain would have been sufficient, but then
the "more" came: Jesus called my name. I still to this day have not
revealed to anyone what I heard; it was not Richard or Richie, but
a name by which Jesus alone knows me.

The experience was like roiling waves, spring storms, and
bursting dams all in the same breath. Like the prophet Isaiah,
it left me a man undone. The little child who heard "Boys don't
cry" throughout his life was then a man sobbing uncontrollably.
It seemed the only response I could make to so great a gift—that
Jesus had died on the cross for me and then called me by name!
The Catholic crucifix finally took on flesh and bone. It was in those
golden moments that I was battered by wave after wave of the
theology of delight, that God not only loves me but also likes me.

I was given a glimpse, an assurance that long ago we wound God's clock for good. It was not that I found the more but rather the more found me. Christianity was not some moral code; it was a love affair, and I had experienced it firsthand.

The intimacy of those three hours exhausted me. I wobbled to my feet, stumbled back to my room, unpacked my bags, and went straight to bed. After that day nothing has ever been the same. I wasn't familiar with the verse then, but it is one I would come to claim and seek to live by, still to this day:

> *There is only Christ: he is everything.*
> Colossians 3:11

In the days that followed my experience in the chapel, I jumped into God with both feet. I completed my undergraduate degree at St. Francis Seminary, with a major in philosophy and a minor in Latin, then spent a year in Washington, D.C., immersed in a spiritual-formation program, followed by four years of advanced theological study at the seminary. And then, on Saturday, May 18, 1963, seven years after finding "more," I was ordained a priest. In a surprisingly tender move, my father and mother hired a bus for family and friends, and they all drove to the cathedral in Altoona, Pennsylvania, for the ordination service. The next morning, Sunday, May 19, I said my first Mass in my old childhood parish, Our Lady of Angels.

The ordination picture stands in contrast to my "cutest baby" photograph. I feel no shame when I look at this one, only a deep

Ordination day, May 18, 1963

and abiding joy, what I have, over the years, called the "happies."

When solemn vows are taken in the Franciscans, the rule is that you must change your first name to a saint's name, an outward symbol of putting on the new man in Christ Jesus. No two men in a community could share the same name; in other words, there couldn't be two Johns or two Michaels. For those who knew me prior to 1963, my name is Richard or Richie. But from that year on, my name has been Brennan.

Part II

BRENNAN

9

There's got to be more. The phrase kept turning and spinning in my head. Such was the case with the Franciscans. I was initially wooed by their life of complete and utter simplicity. But the pope wanted a more educated face on the order, so an emphasis was placed on higher learning, aka, colleges. Through no fault of their own, this move propelled the order into needing everything from clothes to typewriters; in my opinion it was a slouching toward the middle-class that left a bitter taste in my mouth.

In 1966, I sought permission from the Franciscans to take a leave of absence to join the Little Brothers of Jesus. The fraternity is a place where brothers learn to pray together, and in light of the gospel, each man ruthlessly questions himself to discover the path God intends for his life. It is a life of rhythm: singing of the Liturgy of the Hours; celebrating the Eucharist; holy reading (*lectio divina*); and periods of silence, work, and pastoral care. To some it might appear as yet another attempt at a utopian society, but to the brothers themselves it is a lived-out statement that in Jesus Christ such a dream is possible.

My provincial (the equivalent of a bishop for parish priests) denied my request; in fact, he was quite angry that I would even consider leaving the Franciscans. But one lesson I learned in the military was that there is always someone with a higher rank you can appeal to, if you have the guts. So I went over my provincial's head and wrote to the minister general in Rome. His response was, "If this is the call of God on your life, I will honor it. But wait a year." So I impatiently spent the next twelve months teaching and serving as spiritual director at the Franciscan seminary in Loretto. When my year was up, I stepped out into the next stage of my journey.

I would be remiss to talk of the Little Brothers of Jesus without mentioning Charles de Foucauld, the founder of the order, who lived from 1858 to 1916. Foucauld had an experience at the age of twenty-eight, in some ways much like my own, where God broke through and captured his senses. He said, "As soon as I came to believe there was a God, I understood that I could not do otherwise than live only for him."[10] Foucauld made a pilgrimage to the Holy Land and was then ordained as a priest at forty-three.

According to John's gospel, the public ministry of Jesus lasted only three years. Foucauld wondered, *What did He do the other thirty?* The answer he found was that Jesus spent that time in manual labor and prayer. Foucauld realized his own calling in the example of Jesus and set himself to live among the Muslim poor of North Africa, preaching the gospel with his life. For Foucauld and the Little Brothers, life in the desert was not a flight from the world but rather a school of love and prayer to learn to enter more deeply into humanity. Their goal was to shout the gospel not so much with their mouths as with their lives.

After twelve months of waiting, I finally received permission to join the Little Brothers. So in 1967, while my family and friends were busy with their lives in the States, I spent six months in the little village of Saint-Rémy, France. In many ways reminiscent of the Marines, I had stepped into a basic training program. The Brothers referred to my time as "candidacy"—I looked them over, and vice versa, to see if it was a fit.

I spent that winter shoveling manure on nearby farms and washing dishes in a local restaurant. I loved every minute of it. I had no students to counsel or meetings to organize or tests to grade; everything was basic, minimal, and such a breath of fresh air. Evenings were set aside for silence in Eucharistic adoration and meditation on the Scriptures. We did not live a cloistered life in cleric's robes but a plain-clothed existence, contemplatively immersed among the very poor, communicating not through words so much as friendship. We attempted to put Jesus in places where He would normally never be found. We were learning to disengage essentials from nonessentials; not a paradise of solitude, but a place of purging. We lived T. S. Eliot's prayer: "Teach us to care and not to care." A favorite book of mine is Carlo Carretto's *Letters from the Desert*. He summed up well the call each of the Little Brothers responded to. It sounds quite personal because it was.

> Leave everything and come with me into the desert. It is not your acts and deeds that I want; I want your prayer, your love.[11]

My group of Little Brothers was comprised of six men: two Frenchmen, one German, a Spaniard, a Slav, and me. We soon moved on to Farlete, a small village in the Zaragoza desert of Spain. We spent a year of spiritual formation there, known as the novitiate—a season of training and preparation before becoming officially part of the order.

I look back on those times as days of communion—sharing the poverty, toil, and anxiety of rural peasant life alongside the joys of a baby being born, the nuptial bliss of newlyweds, and the small joys of honest work and sweat and cold beer. My primary job was a mason's assistant, a rather lofty title for a builder of chicken coops. This work involved bringing in hundreds of field stones to build the coop and then laying them atop a row of cement, followed by another row of stones, then cement, and so on. It was easily 110 degrees that summer, but I didn't mind it a bit. My other responsibility, and probably the favorite job of my entire life, was that of *aguador* (water carrier). The village didn't have running water, so each morning I would ride out in a donkey-driven buckboard with a water tank in the back. I would later return with the prized possession, water. To say I was popular with the people is an understatement.

One of my realizations in such an earthy atmosphere was that many of the burning theological issues in the church were neither burning nor theological. It was not more rhetoric that Jesus demanded but personal renewal, fidelity to the gospel, and creative conduct. Learning how to build chicken coops and haul water to town benefitted me tremendously in this. But it certainly had its downside. Once I essentially learned the tasks, the days grew long and I grew restless, even in that place I dearly loved.

I remember reading about Yvon Chouinard, the iconic founder of Patagonia, in his book *Let My People Go Surfing*. At one point Chouinard talked of his business rhythm of beginning a new venture, learning the essentials of it, and then moving on to something else. He described it as doing something well to a level of 80 percent and then moving on before reaching 100 percent. When I read those pages, I thought, *That describes so much of my life: Learn it well and then leave it.* My gut tells me that if someone asked Chouinard "Why?" he would answer as I would: *There's got to be more.*

In the Little Brothers, we did have habits, or robes, we would wear only in the chapel. They were a dark gray color embroidered with the *Jesus Caritas* (Jesus Charity) symbol of a red heart with an outcropped cross. One evening while at prayer, wrapped in those threads, I saw my entire life flash before me. This was not like my pretty dream; it was actually rather ugly. I saw my life as vitiated by pride, by the inordinate desire to be liked, loved, approved, applauded, and accepted. Even though I had done well in my desert classroom, my motives were peeled away to reveal complete self-centered yuck. Can you be a self-centered chicken-coop builder? Can a water carrier be stuck on himself? The answer I heard was a resounding and humbling "Yes!" That old desire to be liked reared its ugly head. I thought maybe I had grown beyond it or out of it, but I hadn't.

I was devastated; everything felt Brennan-centered instead of Christ-focused. I felt like my life was a waste, and it made me physically sick. I stood from my ostensibly pious posture of prayer upon hearing an old voice: *He'll never amount to much.* I realize this sounds extreme and like it came out of nowhere, but that's how I recall it. I've had several very clear dreams over the course of my life and my reaction to them has always seemed rash, almost like any dramatic dream demanded an equally dramatic response. So in that moment I determined to commit spiritual suicide, cut myself off from God and the church and the Brothers, turn my back on it all. I didn't know what else I could do. But then someone said, "Hi."

Brother Dominique Voillaume saw my exit from the chapel and asked me what happened. So I told him, told him everything, about my disgust with my own motives and my thoughts of walking away from it all. In that moment he said a powerful thing, a life-changing thing: "You are on the threshold of receiving the greatest grace of your life. You are discovering what it means to be poor in spirit. Brother Brennan, it's okay not to be okay."

My gut reaction was, *This guy's a loon.* But then he led me to the first Beatitude as translated from the New English Bible:

> *How blessed are those who know that they are poor,*
> *the kingdom of Heaven is theirs.*

I've met many people who've told me their doorway to salvation was a hellfire preacher pounding John 3:16. But that's not how it was for me. One of my most memorable lost-then-found moments came via the tender, piercing invitation of a six-foot-two "Little" Brother and Matthew 5:3.

I have written a passage about Brother Dominique Voillaume in my books *Gentle Revolutionaries* (later reissued as *The Importance of Being Foolish*) and *The Signature of Jesus.* I'll repeat that story here, one more time, because I must out of gratitude for the ways his life touched mine and so many others. As this story honors my good friend, it also reveals the inconsistent nature of my life. You see me here one moment about to commit spiritual hara-kiri and the next moment acting like someone who could care less about the ways of God. When I wrote once about "the inconsistent, unsteady disciples whose cheese is falling off their cracker," I was talking about myself.

Mobbed by pigeons in Saint Mark's Square, Venice, March 1968. This photo was taken on a weekend vacation while I was serving with the Little Brothers of Jesus.

There is one day in Saint-Rémy in 1969—New Year's Day to be exact—that my brothers and I would never forget.

We had gathered around our common table, and our talk started out as the standard workman's lament: poor wages, lousy hours, hypocritical employers. Essentially we were singing the blues. But then we rapidly descended into a holier-than-thou rant of comparisons and judgments and how our mammon-loving patrons we selflessly served couldn't possibly compare with the pure-hearted Little Brothers of Jesus. But Brother Dominique sat at the end of our table and began to cry.

"Dominique, please, what is the matter?"

"Ils ne comprennent pas," he said. (Translated, "They don't understand.")

Was my friend and mentor referring to the people we had just verbally maligned, those we saw as oblivious to our mercy while they lounged in bed and made love and drank wine? Or was he actually whispering a prayer for his brothers seated to his right and left, men who had momentarily forgotten our utter poverty before the Father and our kinship with those we so easily condemned? My hope so many, many years later is that his discipline of tears was a covering for us all, a plea of grace streaming to Abba's ears—"Father, forgive them. *Ils ne comprennent pas.*"

Later, Dominique learned he had inoperable cancer and

asked permission to relocate from Saint-Rémy to Paris, where he had close family and relatives. In a move totally unsurprising to those of us who knew him, he took a job as a night watchman in a nearby factory, 11:00 p.m. to 7:00 a.m., the graveyard shift. The story goes that as Dominique would travel home each morning following his shift, he would visit the park across the street from his house, an area filled with what society calls "the riffraff": winos, the old and young and homeless, losers. My good friend traded in his old habit for a new one, that of passing out candy to the least of these, listening to their stories, and always leaving them with good news, words I'd heard a hundred times: "Jesus Christ is crazy about you. He loves you just as you are, not as you should be."

One morning marked the end of Dominique's graveyard shifts. Friends discovered his body on the floor of his flat. The cause of death was determined to be a heart attack. I believe, however, that Dominique died of just the opposite—his was a heart surrender. Here was a man who had surrendered, who had given pieces of his heart to others for a lifetime: a good word here, a gentle touch there, an encouragement always. Dominique's journal was found with this final entry:

> All that is not the love of God has no meaning for me. I can truthfully say that I have no interest in anything but the love of God which is in Christ Jesus. If God wants it to, my life will be useful through my word and witness. If He wants

it to, my life will bear fruit through my prayers and sacrifices. But the usefulness of my life is His concern, not mine. It would be indecent of me to worry about that.

In Little Brothers fashion, Dominique's body was transported down to Saint-Rémy, no embalming. His body was then laid out on a table with a candle at each end. The best phrase I can think of to describe the number of people who came to pay their respects and honor this man is "a great throng." Two of the Little Brothers constructed a simple coffin out of wood, and Dominique's earthly body was buried.

Many times over the years I've wondered why I had the privilege of being friends with Dominique Voillaume, of having my life tenderized by this unsung hero, of being one of thousands at his wake to pause momentarily between the borders of candles and look upon his face. I don't completely know. I do know that his message to me—"It's okay not to be okay"—was a seed that germinated in my later preaching ministry; in fact, it informed everything I wrote and spoke about for more than forty years. Some people might say the line "God loves you as you are, not as you should be" is synonymous with the name Brennan Manning. I would say they're right, but they should know that the truth behind those words was impressed upon me by the life of a man who had experienced it himself. I do know that much. But beyond that, *je ne comprends pas*—I don't understand.

10

After almost two years with the Little Brothers of Jesus in Europe, my internal resistance was too much. I had reached my "80 percent," and it was time to move on to more. I wrote a letter to the Little Brothers, trying to describe my decision. The leader at the time was a generous man named Rene Page. He told me that my letter moved him, and he invited me to the headquarters in Marseille. He also invited four of my closest friends from our novitiate year. We spent a week in prayer and discernment, asking God to reveal my future life in Christ. On the seventh day, we reached a unanimous answer. Ministry was to be a vital dimension in my life, and to neglect it by staying with the Little Brothers would be to run the risk of never becoming myself. To this day, I am so glad I was surrounded by others who could confirm that decision. In contrast to other big decisions I'd made, like entering the military and the seminary, this one felt grounded, and anything grounded is just a little safer.

I was sent to the Franciscan University of Steubenville in Ohio. There I became the campus minister and entered a fascinating season of ministry for me. My primary responsibility was to organize liturgies, prayer meetings, and weekend retreats. Those were days when the Cursillo Movement was at its zenith, a precursor to the Charismatic Renewal in the Catholic Church. The cursillo, or "short course," consisted of taking a group of people away from their normal environment to convey the best news, that Christ loves us, by the best means, friendship. It's still going today and is usually a Thursday through Sunday retreat filled with talks on the essence of Catholic Christianity and the Eucharist. I would regularly take or send five students each weekend to participate.

One of my favorite parts of cursillo is when the veterans of the program who attend the gathering do something called *palanca*, which is Spanish for "to pull a lever and release a power." The lever pulled is prayer; these individuals fast and pray for three days for those engaged in cursillo, without the participants knowing it. On the fourth day, all is revealed, everyone comes together, and there is a very moving closing to the time as each participant steps back into his or her life empowered by the love of Christ. The ultimate goal of cursillo is a living union with God. Had I stayed with the Little Brothers of Jesus, I would have missed being a part of this "more," this season of stirring renewal among both brothers and sisters.

A number of Franciscans on campus were interested in the life I lived among the Little Brothers in Europe; they would sit in rapt attention as I told stories of chicken coops and Brother Dominique. Most of my audience, however, had no interest in leaving the Franciscan order. Living like a Little Brother sounded fun for the weekend, but a life built around such an existence was simply too much.

After two years as the campus minister in Steubenville, I received a proposal for an experimental community in the United States loosely patterned along the same life rhythms as the Little Brothers. To many it sounded like a rather daring proposal; to me it sounded like having your ice cream and eating it too. About thirty men applied for the experiment, and six were selected. I was one of the six and was appointed the leader. We set out to find a place where we could practice living like the Little Brothers here at home in the States.

Left to our own devices, we probably would have struggled to make a decision; we believed too many places in the States would benefit from our experiment. But in the mysterious

economy of grace, we received a call from Bishop John May in
Mobile, Alabama. He was aware of our search and told us of a
boys' home there that had been abandoned because of Hurricane
Camille. If we were interested, we could have it. We went down
to see the property and knew right away it was where we were to
be. The main house was large enough for group gatherings and
meals, and a smaller house was right next door that could accommodate our housing needs. Plus, it was right on the water, in
Bayou La Batre, Alabama, about a mile away from the working
shrimp boats. Brother Luke, our most practical member, said,
"This could work." So with the needed approval, the experimental
Little Brothers moved into what we called "the little place that
could." We had sufficient money for renovation, so we jumped
at the huge task. We completely repainted interior and exterior,
redid the floors, ceiling, and walls, and in seven months everything was ready to go.

Basing everything we did on the pattern of the Little Brothers
of Jesus, we needed to find jobs and be out working among the
people. Thankfully our first jobs came quickly: We worked on
shrimp boats.

When the boats weren't running, we took any jobs we could
find, ranging from housepainters to clerks in hardware stores.
Bishop May's initial question at the outset of our adventure was
"What do you plan to do down there?" But after time passed, that
question evolved into a statement, a commissioning: "Brennan, I
just want you to make it meaningful for the people."

We had no desire to compete with the parish church on

Sunday, so we decided on Friday night celebrations involving the Eucharist at the house, followed by a wine and cheese party. And all those who worked on the shrimp boats could come if they chose. Our services were rather unorthodox from the beginning. We usually got started with a half hour of music, mostly songs from the monks of Weston Priory. This was followed by a message or homily. Gus Gordon, a truly gifted speaker, shared the preaching responsibilities with me. Brother Luke, filled with the gift of hospitality, made sure all other needs were taken care of throughout the time.

One of the first things we purchased in the renovation stage was a huge butcher-block table; it became our altar, our hearth for Communion. I can still remember standing before that table with wine and bread, thinking, *This is right.*

We adorned the walls of the house with nautical motifs so the people felt at home there, and in no time at all, we did too. Over the course of two years, we had more than two hundred people coming on Friday nights, people who had not been to church in years. Some called what we were doing "the folk Mass." Seeing as how we were living with and among beautiful common folk, I had no problem with that. In fact, I liked it a lot.

Then a huge wrench was thrown into our ministry. After two years, the Franciscan community in Pennsylvania deemed our experiment a failure. I never received any deeper explanation. Maybe if we'd had more official converts, but the bottom line is I don't know the reason. What I do know is that our every move was based on the Little Brothers' spirit of taking Christ to the people, not the other way around. So we had no regrets. After our community dispersed, Gus said to me, "Brennan, that was the richest experience of my life." I looked into my friend's tear-filled eyes and affirmed, "Gus, it was one of my happiest."

II

My story up to this point has followed a loose chronology—one thing happening after the other. But for the rest of this section, time will loop, even fold over on itself. It's strange how things can go from happy to sad so quickly. But they can. The paragraphs that follow deal with some very dark days in regard to my alcoholism. I don't even really know how to talk about it. Some of that is due to the shame I feel and some of that is because of the toll alcohol has taken on my mind.

The medical name for it is Wernicke-Korsakoff syndrome; I know it as "wet brain." It has to do with a thiamine deficiency brought about by poor nutritional habits; in other words, the person replaces food with alcohol. Over time this deficit causes significant brain-cell death. One of the telling signs of this syndrome is mental confusion, sometimes to the point of insisting upon events that did not happen. So you can imagine why I approach telling you about these days with hesitation.

To me, the experiment in Bayou La Batre was like an extended summer vacation. And what do you do when summer's over? Go back to class, which I did. I became the campus minister at Broward Community College in Fort Lauderdale, Florida. There were days at Broward when I experienced more than I could imagine, and then there were days of more than I could handle. It was a time of intense loneliness. Oh, I enjoyed the college students; in fact, I feel I've always been able to connect well with that age group. But I had just come out of this idyllic experience in Bayou La Batre surrounded by a close-knit group of peers and suddenly that all went away.

Thinking about it now, the students of Broward were a decent reflection of my life at the time. Some of the students were passing with flying colors, winning awards, and gathering acclaim. I experienced days like that at Broward, moments of being on top of the world. Some faculty members verbally affirmed my presence on campus, and I enjoyed favor in the eyes of the administration. But other students on campus were just getting by, barely passing, skipping as many classes as possible, and doing only the minimum required. I knew how to do that too. I learned what was expected of me and learned what I could get away with. To say "I was spending time in prayer" was sometimes true but other times merely a spiritual facade to cover my laziness.

And then there were the students not just struggling but failing to the degree that their entire career plans were at risk and they might not graduate on time, if at all. They were disappointing the ones closest to them, but more importantly they were diminishing themselves and were often too stubborn to ask for help. It wasn't that way for me in the beginning at Broward, but I got there soon. Beyond the required duties on campus, I had a lot of time on my hands and I didn't have any chicken coops to build or shrimp nets to mend or houses to paint. There was just me and something that had soothed my insecurities in the past: alcohol. We often go back to what we know, and that's not always a good thing.

In that year and a half or so in Fort Lauderdale, I started drinking again. Now, it wasn't that I had ever really stopped drinking; having a few beers with friends or wine with meals was commonplace for me. But what resumed in Florida was reminiscent of when my habit began as a sixteen-year-old boy, back when my nickname was Funnel. You're probably still wondering why or how this could happen. The Trappist monk Thomas Keating once said, "The cross Jesus asked you to carry is yourself. It's all the pain inflicted on you in your past and all the pain you've inflicted on others." I believe that's true. My cross suddenly became too heavy, and I couldn't carry it. I just couldn't.

Although I have always given the appearance of speaking openly about my alcoholism, rest assured it has always been only what I wanted the listener or reader to know, nothing more. I will never be able to tell all in regard to that part of my story. But I do want to try to represent some of it here if possible, maybe as a backdrop. It feels like a weak attempt, but maybe it indicates the thick darkness that was always behind any light in my life. I thought about creating a chart where I indicated how much I drank during that cross-heavy season, but that felt cold and clinical. Besides, real life's not a chart but a story. So here's a story that I believe tells you what you need to know.

After a year and a half at Broward, my drinking was out of control. I had started my time there by drinking Sundays through Wednesdays, a schedule that gave me plenty of time to be sober by the weekend. I was frequently invited to speak in churches on the weekends, and I never wanted to disgrace the ministry by showing up intoxicated. No, the utter hypocrisy of that is not lost on me.

As time went on, my boundaries loosened and alcohol spilled over into every day of the week. And in 1975, at the age of forty-one,

I found myself a patient at Hazelden, a rehab center in Center City, Minnesota. I cannot remember all the details of how and why I got there, but I do remember something about *once* I got there.

I told this story in my book *The Ragamuffin Gospel*. It is about a man named Max—one in our group of twenty-five chemically dependent men—and our counselor, a senior member of the Hazelden staff named Sean Murphy-O'Connor. A part of the official recovery process was that each man had to take his turn in the hot seat, being the focus of intense questioning by O'Connor and the other members of the group. Although necessary to get at the root of the individual's problem, this experience was incredibly painful for everyone.

O'Connor ruthlessly questioned Max about his drinking habits and how he rationalized his behavior. Eventually, Max finally became worn down and admitted that he hid bottles of vodka and gin in everything from nightstands to medicine cabinets to suitcases. Max followed his admission by stating the Bible verse about specks in your brother's eyes and planks in your own; his air of smug self-confidence was nothing short of offensive. O'Connor pressed further by calling up Max's friends and family and asking them about his drinking, but Max continued justifying his drinking behavior to the point of standing in a rage and unleashing a string of profanities at O'Connor.

Finally, Max was asked if he'd ever been unkind to one of his children. O'Connor called Max's wife and she revealed a night when Max went in to have a few drinks with his buddies and left his daughter in the car in freezing temperatures. His daughter's ears and fingers were badly frostbitten, resulting in the need for amputation of a thumb and permanent hearing loss. Max collapsed on all fours and began to sob, reduced to the ground of his lies and deceptions. O'Connor said, "Get out of here…. I'm not running a rehab for liars."

But what I've never revealed about that story is how much I envied Max in that time. Let me try to explain. Max went through the eye of the needle in that experience, but he came out on the other side a different man. His demeanor changed, almost overnight, and I truly believe he found God. I had my own time in the hot seat with O'Connor, and he brought all of his skills to that moment, lovingly trying to break me. But I wouldn't break. I was never receptive to the tough-love approach, even though I've applauded it in print. It's easy to approve of something when it's not being done to you.

I would love to tell you that one day in Hazelden I was on my knees in the center of the room sobbing hysterically, owning up to my drinking and lies. But that never happened. Max left the treatment center a broken man but also a changed man. I left the center known as "a tough nut to crack." I was clean and sober but far from honest.

While at Hazelden, part of our curriculum was to give peer reviews. The purpose of peer reviews was, as Hazelden put it, to offer our peers help in seeing themselves more specifically, their areas of dishonesty, their defense mechanisms, and their character defects. It takes courage to risk confronting. We have all traded our honesty for the approval of others in the past. However, if we care about our fellow peers, and if we want them to be honest with us in return, we will present them with our picture of them. Our disease is life-threatening. Recovery requires taking risks, learning about ourselves, and making changes.

Here is an example of a peer-review worksheet we all had to fill out. I've kept it as a keepsake of sorts, of how bad things can really get.

A. I SEE YOU DOING THE FOLLOWING TO PRESENT BARRIERS TO YOUR RECOVERY (circle statements which apply)
1. I don't see you participating in group without prodding
2. I hear you trying to patch everyone up in the community
3. I see you feeling that you deserve special treatment
4. I hear you talking down to other patients on the unit

5. I see you full of denial (minimizing, explaining, justifying)

6. I see you hiding in anger

7. I see you acting like an "old pro" in treatment

8. I see you playing counselor

9. I see you being self-controlled

10. I see you trying to manage the unit

11. I see you not accepting your addiction

12. I hear you bragging about your addiction (war stories)

13. I hear you talking one way in group and another way in community

B. I SEE YOU USING THE FOLLOWING DIVERSIONS TO KEEP FROM DEALING WITH YOUR DISEASE (circle statements which apply)

1. Watching TV, playing cards or games, etc

2. Preoccupied with everything but treatment

3. Using self-pity (PLOM—poor little old me)

4. Getting romantically involved, flirting, etc

5. Preoccupied and talking about physical problems

6. People pleasing

7. Using humor/joking to keep from showing true feelings

8. Staying alone (isolating)

Out of all the Hazelden peers who filled out this form for me, every one of them circled all twenty-one items. I received a horribly perfect score. Then again, I'd had almost a decade of consistent practice, and practice makes perfect.

I don't like to discuss my time at Hazelden. It was one of the most challenging experiences in all my life, and many times I didn't know if I had the strength to face it. But I did face it, albeit imperfectly. In addition to being a dreamer, I was a survivor, much like my mother. I could grit my teeth and make it. My mother left her bruised decade, got the education she needed, and worked hard to succeed. I followed that same approach and began writing in earnest my life's message of grace. My mother also found someone to marry after her bruised decade. Like my mother, I did too.

Roslyn and me

12

I'm sure you've gathered by now that I live with plenty of regrets. But my greatest regret is that I did not know how to be married. Remembering that time in my life, even now, feels like touching a tender wound. I have not written about those days—they have not been the stuff of conference talks or books. But I will write about them now.

As you know, I was raised in an Irish-Catholic family. Even with
the difficulties I experienced with my parents, my decision to enter
the priesthood was met with great approval. It was not a lateral
move in my family of origin but a vertical leap. I moved up in my
parents' estimation. And in binding myself by the Franciscan vow,
I was unable to contract a valid marriage. To transgress this vow in
any way would be a grievous sin. I was bound by the choice I had
freely made.

After I left Hazelden and began taking speaking engagements, my star began to rise. At the time, a priest willing to talk
about his alcoholism in one breath and God's unconditional love
in the next was out of the ordinary. I was being invited to speak
more and more. One such request was for a weekend retreat in
Morgan City, Louisiana.

The town slogan of Morgan City was "right in the middle
of everywhere." At the time, I had no way of knowing how much
that slogan fit my experience there. But now I do. It was there
that I first met Roslyn, right in the middle of the everything and
everywhere of my life. I was in my early forties, and I felt clean and
hopeful, like anything could happen.

The retreats I spoke at usually kept to a structure: After the
formal time of speaking, attendees were offered an opportunity to
visit for a bit of pastoral counseling. People lined up to chat with
me.

Roslyn prefaced her time slot with, "I'm not sure why I'm
here—I really don't have any problems." But as I soon learned, she
was a mess, just like me.

I gave Roslyn the name of a prayer group that met in New Orleans with the feeling that it would be a good group for her, a place for support and guidance. I knew some of the members of the prayer group; I trusted them and met with them when I could. By that time I had relocated to New Orleans, having always loved the city.

In those fifteen or twenty minutes together with Roslyn, I learned that she was a single mother with two daughters, that she had been raised in a Baptist-Catholic home, her father the former, her mother the latter. She had one brother two years older, Michael, whom she dearly loved and who was killed in 1969 while flying a night mission in Laos, a tragedy she's understandably never gotten over.

After our brief conversation, that was it; she walked out and the next in line sat down. The next face could have been Hank Aaron's or even Gerald Ford's, but I wouldn't have noticed. My head was filled with the shapely form of the runner-up to the Miss San Antonio pageant of 1962, better known as Roslyn.

Back in New Orleans, she joined the prayer group that gathered regularly. She met friends of mine, and they met her. About a year later, Roslyn invited the prayer group to a crawfish boil at her home. She thought to invite me as well. It's possible I recommended Roslyn to that prayer group because I thought it might mean seeing her again. I really don't think of myself as that suave, but it's possible. One of Roslyn's gifts is hospitality. She knows how to host well, and as such, the evening turned out grand. Whether by my offer or her request, I found myself helping her clean up after dinner, carrying some things out to the garage. It was then and there the priest and the lady found themselves in a kiss. It wasn't that we didn't like it; I believe we did. I know I did. But we sure hadn't planned on it. I intentionally wrote "in a kiss" instead of "we kissed." That first kiss led us "in"—into an experience of feeling like we were right in the middle of everything. I was scared to death.

After that, I would call Roslyn when I was in town. She would pick me up on her lunch hour, and soon enough, our meetings became as predictable as humidity in New Orleans: Get take-out po'boy sandwiches, head to the lakefront area of Lake Pontchartrain, eat our lunch, and then play what I have always liked to call kissy-face and huggy-bear. The word *halcyon* denotes a period of time in the past that was idyllically happy and peaceful. I remember those Pontchartrain getaways as halcyon days.

During one of our noontime get-togethers, we said *the* words, yes, *those* words: "I love you." Foolish words for a celibate priest? Maybe. But as Erasmus said,

> The greatest part of mankind are fools … and friendship, you know, is seldom made but amongst equals.

Roslyn and I talked on the phone a great deal in those days—on rotary phones with long cords. We also saw each other

as often as we could, all depending on my schedule. I was basically speaking full-time and traveling constantly, so we saw each
other only about once every two to three months. Our relationship
continued that way for almost seven years. And then one day when
we were together, Roslyn said, "I don't want to see you anymore."

It would be many years later that Roslyn would tell me that
in the beginning of our relationship, she had promised herself she
would not ask me to choose between her and the priesthood. She
kept that promise; she never asked. But seven years is a long time
for anyone to live apart from the person he or she loves, playing
second fiddle to God.

But what could I do? I was a Franciscan priest vowed to
the celibate life. Roslyn was a single mother. We were in love. If
our lives had been a movie musical accompanied by a Rodgers
and Hammerstein score, it might have worked. We could have
just sung about a few of our favorite things—po'boys and New
Orleans—and then maybe we wouldn't have felt so bad. But ours
was the classic forbidden love story, the kind always resolved by
some version of death.

We decided to have no contact for two months. After that
time, we would meet and talk. Those two months were hell for
me; I'm sure they gave me a taste of what Roslyn had lived with for
years. When we met, I told her my decision. I would take a leave
of absence from my ministry and enter into a time of discernment
concerning our relationship. In a very real sense, discernment is a
process of finding the "best fit." I decided to take a year away and
seek the life that fit.

So off I went, once again, to monastery walls. Although not in a formal setting like mine, Roslyn assured me she would also spend that time seeking the right thing to do. I realize that discernment stuff all sounds überspiritual; the truth is that it was the longest, most heart-wrenching year of my life.

On March 12, 1966, an article was published in the *Saturday Evening Post* titled "I Am a Priest, I Want to Marry" under the name Father Stephen J. Nash. The article questioned the practice of celibacy among priests and was written under a pseudonym. The public response to the article was a mix of celebration and rage, which fueled a demand for the real author to reveal his true identity. A courageous young priest by the name of James Kavanaugh stood up, and soon enough, he took the seeds of the article and wrote the book *A Modern Priest Looks at His Outdated Church*.

Here's a little bit of context. About four years earlier, as part of a speech led by Pope John XXIII, nearly three thousand bishops gathered in Rome to "open the stained-glass windows and let in some fresh air"—also known as Vatican II. The changes set in motion were revolutionary, allowing the laity the freedom to celebrate the Mass in their own language and to have their priest facing the congregation instead of the altar. It was very much a move to empower the people and to turn spectators into participants and observers into celebrants. Many people experienced a freedom, some of them for the first time, to think for themselves, question anything, wrestle with ideas, or, as I've liked to say, "stretch their minds." Married priests was one of those stretching issues, but to the Vatican, the conversation had taken the idea of freedom too far.

So in October 1967, while concluding his lecture at Notre Dame University before a room of budding theologians, Kavanaugh removed his collar and publicly announced his resignation from the priesthood. It was a shocking move that brought the house to its feet. One week later, the Notre Dame Alumni Association took out a full-page ad in the *New York Times* in an attempt to tame the "enthusiastic approval" from the public. Kavanaugh's publisher offered him a half-page counter ad. He accepted the offer and wrote:

> I am resigning from the Catholic priesthood in personal protest against the refusal of the hierarchy of the institutional Church to bring about reform.... I can no longer wear the collar nor accept the title of "Father," when the institution I represent can cut off from communion the divorced and remarried, can refuse to admit its error in the matter of birth control, can ignore the plea of priests for marriage, can continue to reduce the principles of Christ to instruments of fear and guilt.... I cannot continue to be identified with a power structure that permits only token changes while the screams of millions are not heard.[12]

In his book, Kavanaugh further explained:

> If I were to leave the priesthood because celibacy
> makes no sense and hides the very Christian love
> it once was meant to serve, I would be a renegade,
> a traitor, a man without a home. I would still be a
> priest, but a wretched and lonely one, adrift from
> family and friends. If I were to marry, my parents
> would be asked to ignore the wife I chose....
> They would reject me, the son who made them
> proud and happy, the son who wants to do it still.
> They would turn away and offer all their misery
> to God. They would sneak to Church, avoid the
> pastor, fear each conversation that could whisper
> of their shame, and wonder where they failed in
> their labors for my life.[13]

It was 1981, I was a forty-seven-year-old priest, and I wanted
to marry as well. So at the end of my twelve months apart from
Roslyn, after a season of discerning, it was time for a decision. My
earlier vows deemed it a sin to marry. I had been warned. But in
those twelve months, it had become clear to me that the formal
priesthood no longer fit; the greater sin would be *not* to marry. I
had more than one Franciscan friend encourage me to request to
be laicized, or given lay status. This is an official title in the church

that essentially means being defrocked, stripped of priestly function and privilege. In my particular situation, taking on this status would have meant agreeing to these three terms:

1. I had never had the calling to be a priest.
2. I had lost my vocation.
3. I had been seduced.

If I had agreed to these terms, I would have remained in good standing within the church and might have had a slim possibility to continue my preaching and teaching ministry within. But those terms simply were not true. I could not, with any sense of integrity, give my consent.

Another sense of the word *discernment* is "a cutting away." In order to fit into my new life, I realized I could not merely be laicized. I could not agree to the untrue qualifications, which meant that getting to where I wanted—to be married—would require a metaphorical cutting away from my vocation as a priest.

> *And if your right hand should cause you to sin,*
> *cut it off and throw it away; for it will do you less*
> *harm to lose one part of you than to have your*
> *whole body go to hell.*
>
> Matthew 5:30

13

I phoned Roslyn on Easter Sunday of 1982 and told her of my decision, that *not* to marry would be the greater sin, a refusal of the gift God had given me in her. I then asked her, over the phone, to marry me. She said, "Yes, Brennan, I will." I can still hear her answer in my head; they were beautiful words. My old dream had been for someone to come along and say, "I like you. Can we play together?" The spirit of Roslyn's response was the same. "I like you. Let's grow old together." Her answer gave me an extended case of the happies. I wish everyone we knew would have been that happy for us, but they weren't.

At the time, I was booked out for two years' worth of speaking engagements, more than two hundred accepted invitations. Once my formal letter of resignation reached the archdiocese, all my speaking engagements were canceled. I was no longer welcome in the Catholic diocese in New Orleans. During that time, Roslyn was employed by one of the churches in New Orleans, working in their religious education program. She resigned before she was fired. All of this didn't happen overnight, but it felt like it. Emotional time is often compressed. We were now the renegades, the traitors, the couple without a home, adrift from most family and many friends.

About six months later, with less than ten thousand dollars between the two of us, we got married. It was a small gathering in a friend's home, and Dr. Francis MacNutt, a trusted colleague, officiated our ceremony. To my knowledge, the photographs contained in this book are the only ones that exist from our wedding. I remember the complete support of Roslyn's mother, a beautiful woman who welcomed me with open arms. But I also remember that a few friends didn't show up. They simply could not, in good conscience, be a part of approving our union. They weren't the only ones.

James Kavanaugh's words spoke to the weight of shame that a family would bear if their priest-son decided to marry. This held true for my family of origin. My parents and my sister did not attend our wedding ceremony; it was just too much. There is a part of me that cannot understand that, yet there is now another part that does. They had seen me go from budding scholar to soldier to seminarian to priest; I had reached a pinnacle, and now I was throwing it all away. But in a bold move that spoke volumes to me, something I will never forget, my brother showed up via train and surprised us a few days after the wedding. I will never forget Rob's support in that way. He always was tuff.

Dr. Francis MacNutt officiating our wedding

138   BRENNAN MANNING

After years of the celibate life, I was now married. I sincerely felt God's approval of our marriage. The discernment process had helped me say, "We're supposed to be together, Roslyn," because God had said, "You're supposed to be together, Brennan." I didn't believe it would be easy, but I did believe it was right. Added to being a husband, I was now a stepfather to two daughters, sixth-grader Simone and high-school freshman Nicole. I went from being Father Brennan Manning to father Brennan Manning. Most of my adult life had been spent in the close proximity of men—priests, brothers. Now I was living under the same roof with three women. Talk about being dazed; I had no idea what I was supposed to do. I cannot speak authoritatively for old dogs, but teaching middle-aged priests new tricks is quite the challenge. A fly on the wall would have seen me basically continuing to do what I'd always done—read, pray, observe daily Mass, write—just now in mixed company.

As I said, I was dismissed from the order and my tank full of speaking engagements suddenly went dry. A year into our marriage, Roslyn and I were down to about a thousand dollars in the bank, and tuition payments for the girls' school were coming up. I didn't know what to do, and the voices of shame and guilt were gaining steam. My desire to provide for my family was being thwarted. Those were days of learning the reality behind the phrase I've often used, "ruthless trust." It's something easy to say but much harder to live. But I have learned in my life that grace often gestates, like an unborn child. And when the expectant mother grabs the hospital-prepared suitcase and screams, "Let's go!" then you'd better go.

In the spring of 1983, I received a phone call from a man in Billings, Montana. He wondered if I would be interested in coming and giving a series of talks. He had heard some of my taped talks. It sounded rather unorganized, but it promised some income so I agreed. He took out an ad in the local paper and convinced an Assembly of God pastor to host the event. The first day, I spoke to almost a thousand people. The second day, we had twelve hundred. By the last night, we had a crowd of fifteen hundred people. The pastor said, "Brennan, you Catholics don't know how to ask for money, so let me make an appeal." His words were very biblical about supporting those who preach the gospel; I remember feeling deeply moved and appreciated. The collection was taken, and I returned to New Orleans with a check for fifteen thousand dollars. When I handed Roslyn the check, she had to sit down.

Three weeks later I received a phone call from Bob Krulish, the director for Young Life in the Rocky Mountain region. Bob had heard me speak as a priest back in 1968 at Calvary Community Church in San Jose and had evidently seen and heard something he liked. He called to ask if I would speak at their annual staff- and leadership-training weekend at Glen Eyrie in Colorado Springs. I didn't come home with a check for fifteen thousand, but I did okay. That weekend began a long tenured relationship of speaking and ministering to the leadership and staff of Young Life.

Then one week later I received a call from a man named Mike Yaconelli. Mike was the life force behind the Youth Specialties ministry. He had scheduled a conference speaker, who had canceled, and asked if I could possibly come and speak in her place. I agreed. Once again, the money didn't rival Billings', but the time I spent there was beyond rich, and that experience began my long and notorious friendship with the "beautiful sinner," Mike Yaconelli.

Those three phone calls were the rebirth of my speaking ministry, and they happened one after the other, just like that. Those opportunities were an affirmation of my deepest calling as an evangelist, a shot-in-the-arm of encouragement that I sorely needed at the time. They were also a truckload of assurances to Roslyn, obviously in the financial sense, but much more in the sense that God had not abandoned us. Yes, it's an evil generation that keeps asking for signs, but a tangible sign of God's approval every once in a while can bolster your courage for months, not to mention pay the bills.

14

I want to share three small movements that happened during my life with Roslyn: the good, the not-so good, and the ugly. There was the initial honeymoon phase, followed by the settling in, and then the creeping distance. I said earlier that my greatest regret in life is not knowing how to be married. That's true, but in no way do I regret trying.

The Good.

I enjoyed my new life, I really did. I chose it, and much about it was good, very good. We lived in a wonderful house in New Orleans at the time, a house well suited for entertaining, which we did often. The house was just down the street from where Roslyn's mother lived. As I've said, Roslyn was the consummate hostess; she knew how to throw things together in a moment's notice. That was good because she quickly realized that "a moment" was about all I would often give her. I was constantly inviting people into our home on the spur of the moment—to visit, celebrate Mass, or join us for dinner. I loved the feel of a house filled with chatter and the smell of food; maybe that was a carryover from my days in Alabama. It was not uncommon for Roslyn to have no idea who this or that person was; sometimes I didn't either. Our house was more than a house; it was a hearth, a safe place for people to gather. And there were flowers, always flowers. Roslyn had the gift of arranging azaleas and petunias and begonias and yellow mums around our house so that even the grounds were a gracious invitation.

If my stepdaughters were asked about my fathering skills, they might laugh. I might too. But those girls were definitely part of the "good" in our marriage. I could bless the host in our daily Mass, but as to what to do with two teenage girls, I didn't have a clue. They were very gracious to accept me and share their mother with me. I hope they have some memories filed under "good" too. I quoted Richard Rohr earlier about shame being transferred if it isn't transformed. I had an awareness of this and intentionally tried to do some things with the girls so as not to repeat the sins of the past.

One thing that was missing in the girls' lives was a sense of celebration around birthdays, or at least I thought so. I wanted them to know how very special they were. That was something I had not experienced on my birthdays, so it was a variation of doing unto others as I wish had been done to me. Our celebrations would extend before and beyond the actual birthday. We created a new tradition: The birthday girl—this included Roslyn—could pick out any restaurant in New Orleans she wanted, and we'd go there for a dress-up, sit-down, way-too-many-forks, expensive dinner. I loved to give them gifts, and in retrospect, I probably gave too much. I've never loved money; it hasn't mattered to me personally. However, I've enjoyed it in the sense that it allowed me to shower gifts on those closest to me. I honestly do not believe I was trying to buy their love but rather express mine in a way I could. I've heard my stepdaughters carry on the birthday tradition in their own families, in their own ways. Those birthday celebrations are some of my fondest memories.

I do have to mention two other family members as being among the "good." They were our dogs: Binky, a Pomeranian, and Maxwell, a Yorkie. I was closer to Binky. It drove Roslyn and the girls crazy when I wouldn't discipline him when he misbehaved, but I always felt the poor guy just needed a lot of grace. I finished many evenings by watching a little television, and Binky was always there, right by my side. I have to confess, it's amazing how close you can feel to a dog.

The Not-So Good.

At our home in New Orleans, we had a swimming pool, an aspect of our home that everyone enjoyed, including me. But an outdoor swimming pool must be cleaned regularly. It's a chore. One day Roslyn asked me to clean it. I tried, but I did a shoddy job. Roslyn asked me again about it later, and I replied, "No, I won't do it. It's disturbing my peace of mind!" Yes, I really said that. I went inside, and Roslyn ended up cleaning the pool. This one event serves as an apt metaphor: Roslyn and I were married for eighteen years, and for most of those, while I was traveling and preaching and writing and cultivating my peace of mind, Roslyn cleaned the pool.

Many personality inventories were available to us, complete with grids and questions designed to help a man or woman or married couple on their journeys of self-discovery. Roslyn and I both spent time with and benefitted from the Enneagram. I know that some people believe the Enneagram is dangerous, with roots in the occult. But I don't agree with that assessment. Probably one of the best-known advocates of the Enneagram is Father Richard Rohr, a man I greatly admire and respect.

Here's how the inventory goes: Following a series of subtle and complex questions, your basic personality type is identified. There are nine types that correspond to a number 1–9. Roslyn is a 1, which is "the Reformer"—purposeful and self-controlled. I am a 4, "the Individualist"—self-absorbed and temperamental. The nine types are further divided into Centers—Instinctive (1, 8, 9), Feeling (2, 3, 4), and Thinking (5, 6, 7)—and then further clarified by the dominant emotion in each Center: Anger/Rage (1, 8, 9), Shame (2, 3, 4), and Anxiety (5, 6, 7). Here are two brief descriptions of those dominant emotions, based on our results:

> **Ones** attempt to control or repress anger. They feel it imperative to stay in control of their impulses and anger at all times.

> **Fours** attempt to control shame by focusing on how unique and special they are. They emphasize their individuality and creativity in order to deal with feelings of inadequacy. And they manage their shame by creating a vibrant fantasy life where they do not have to deal with the mundane things of life.

It is said a relationship/marriage between a 1 and a 4 is like combining oil and water. Throw alcohol into that mix and the question is not if problems will arise, but when and how they will be weathered.

So take the pool example, for instance, in light of the Enneagram numbers. I, being a 4, felt my inner sanctum of peace, where the "brilliance of Brennan Manning" was cultivated and was of paramount importance, was disturbed. Being bothered by something so mundane as cleaning the pool was simply an intrusion into greatness. Yes, that's incredibly arrogant, I know. But it's how I felt. Couple that with Roslyn being a 1 and the frustration she felt at me for not being willing to be a part of the human race. But she wanted to stay in control, so her tendency was to repress the anger, redirect the energy around that situation, and then just go do it herself. I said something about when and how our problems were "weathered." Days when the pool needed to be cleaned may have been sunny on the outside, but inside they were partly cloudy with a chance of storms. The Enneagram didn't help us solve these dilemmas necessarily, but it at least gave us an awareness and a language to use to discuss them.

The Ugly.

I said our home was more than just a home—it was a hearth, a place of warmth and safety. The Greek word *eschara* means fireplace or hearth. The hearth was traditionally found in the middle of the house, the axis around which most domestic activities took place. It was where parents and children gathered. As such, it was also where many injuries took place because of the open nature of the hearth's structure; in other words, it's where you got burned. You can't have the hearth without the risk of scars.

But an abundance of scarring leaves scar tissue, skin inferior to normal, healthy skin. The damaged tissue is limited in its functions, including movement, circulation, and sensation. It's one thing if that happens to a hand or arm or leg. It's something else altogether if that repeatedly happens to the heart.

At the peak of my speaking ministry I began a game with Roslyn, with myself, and even with God. It was an adult version of my childhood game Ringolevio—hide and come find me. I often overscheduled myself, allowing only a few days between speaking engagements that were usually on opposite coasts. The rules of my game were these: I would finish the engagement, get a hotel room near the airport, close myself in, and drink. I wouldn't call Roslyn, or anyone for that matter, to "check in." This seclusion might last for one to four days. And there you have it: hide and come find me, a child's game played by a grown man.

Roslyn picked up on my game and was almost always able to track me down. A phone call would follow with pleas: "Brennan, please come home." I would return to New Orleans, and our hearth would then backdrop the excruciating physical process of an alcoholic's withdrawals. Roslyn tried as best she could to shield the girls from those times, but I believe they knew something was wrong. If they couldn't tell it by looking at me, they could sure tell it by looking at Roslyn; the toll was beginning to show in her eyes. One of the realities of the family of an alcoholic is that they often get sucked into the craziness themselves. No one intends for this to happen, it just does. This happened to Roslyn. At her own admission, at times she was in as much denial as I was; in our own individual ways we strained to hide the truth and keep up appearances. What is there in life that can prepare you to live with an alcoholic? I don't think there's anything; you find yourself in that situation and do your best, and that's what Roslyn did.

My "best" game, so to speak, was a nine-day disappearance. No one knew where I was. At the time, Roslyn was doing some post-grad work at Loyola, working toward a master's degree in religious education. My disappearance was so intense and anxiety-filled for her that she dropped out for that semester. She did complete her degree, seven years later, no doubt because she didn't have to spend all of her time looking for me. Our marriage was suffering, and it was affecting everything.

I finally phoned, telling her I was heading home. I don't remember her saying anything during that phone call (what could she have said?). Nevertheless, she met me at the airport, not the winsome-rag-pants-storytelling me, but the reeking-of-vomit-drunken me who could hardly breathe. My lungs were the first to be affected by those stretches of drinking; respiratory problems were consistently a part of my withdrawals. In that particular scene I had such difficulty breathing that she rushed me to the ER at Ochsner Hospital. After sufficient time to dry out, I was released with some meds and sent home. A few days later I was back on a plane, headed to my next speaking engagement and another round of Brennan Manning's Ringolevio.

Marriage by definition involves two people, not one. There are always two sides to every story, and the truth often hovers somewhere between the two. Roslyn had angels and demons she wrestled with, just like I did. I don't believe there was some singular moment when we realized things were ugly. It was a progression, a gradual accretion, a number of moments between a 1 and a 4 that if marriage was a formula might result in a 5. But marriage, like life I believe, is not an equation. Sometimes things just don't add up.

> In those years, people will say, we lost track
> of the meaning of we, of you
> we found ourselves
> reduced to I

> Adrienne Rich, "In Those Years"

We were married for sixteen years, and then we separated in
1998. After a year, we tried to reunite, but it was obvious that the
tissue of our marriage was fatally scarred, the damage was done,
and we were both pretty numb. A year later, in 2000, our divorce
was final. Including those seven years of kissy-face and huggy-bear
before marriage, Roslyn and I were together for a total of twenty-
five years. And then we were not.

Me, Roslyn, my sister-in-law, Celie, and my brother, Rob

15

To live in this world you must be able to do three things:
To love what is mortal;
To hold it against your bones knowing your life depends on it;
And, when the time comes to let it go, to let it go.[14]

Mary Oliver, "In Blackwater Woods"

I didn't know how to be married, but following our divorce, I discovered I didn't know how *not* to be married. So maybe I did know and just didn't know it. There I go, in my head again, intellectualizing a matter of the heart. But nowadays, those semantic puzzles make my brain hurt, and they do little to honor the thread of grace that runs through our relationships and our attempts, however feeble, to love one another. So what remained after our marriage ended? We did, I guess.

I can see something in my mind's eye, though, a scarred image that both gnaws at me and calms me. I see flowers.

I think of Paul Harding's *Tinkers*:

> The field was an abandoned lot. The remnants of an old house, long since fallen into ruin, stood at the back of the field. The flowers must have been the latest generation of perennials, whose ancestors were first planted by a woman who lived in the ruins when the ruins were a raw, unpainted house inhabited by herself and a smoky, serious husband and perhaps a pair of silent, serious daughters, and the flowers were an act of resistance against the raw, bare lot with its raw house sticking up from the raw earth like an act of sheer, inevitable, necessary madness because human beings have to live somewhere and in something…. So the flowers were maybe a balm or, if not a balm, some sort of gesture signifying the balm she would apply were it in her power to offer redress.[15]

16

The last few years leading up to our divorce tore my emotions to shreds. I was traveling way too much, isolated and drunk. On the surface it appeared I was doing well. But below the surface loneliness and insecurity churned with a merciless fury. I sincerely don't know that my speaking was very valuable during those years. People told me the talks were life changing and the books were liberating, but I just don't know. I did make one decision I'll never regret though: hanging out with some good men.

I felt more alone than I had in years. I longed for the days like I'd experienced with the Little Brothers, a male camaraderie I

knew could be a reality. So I sent an invitation out to a group of
men who knew me but didn't know one another, men with names
like Paul and Alan and Devlin and Bob and Butch and John and
Fil and Mickey and Mike and Gene and Ed and John and Lou
and John Peter. I think that was in 1993, but I'm not certain. I've
asked them and have gotten differing answers, but the bottom line
is we don't care what year is was, only that it happened. Most of
the men I had met at retreats and conferences over the years. A few
knew me only by way of my books or taped messages, but we had
corresponded by phone or mail. The invite was simple: Join me for
a few days in Mississippi. I don't believe the invitation elaborated
further as to what we might do. As I look at that now, I see traces
of my old dream, the only difference being this time I was the one
taking the initiative: "I like you. Can we hang out together?"

They all said yes, or as one of them later said, "We were the
only ones crazy enough to say yes." I was thrilled and scared to
death. On one level, a roomful of men is always a dangerous thing.
Competition is usually in the air, so the potential for violence
is always nearby. Strutting and jockeying for position are rather
frequent occurrences too. But there was a common denomina-
tor among these men, one of the reasons I invited them and not
others. It was something I shared too—we were all broken. My
prayerful hope was that this might shield us from the usual male
shenanigans.

I was nervous on another level too though. I had impressed
these men from the stage or in the pages of a book as Brennan
Manning. But now I would be in the same room with them for

several days as equals. I wasn't sure I knew how to be just Brennan, and I didn't know if they would like just Brennan.

Our first meeting was nothing short of beautiful. There is a tendency toward transparency and vulnerability these days that did not exist back then, or if it did it was rare, especially among men. A few of the men saw right away this experience wasn't for them, and they left, not to return. That was fine. But for those of us who stayed, the weekend was like water to the thirsty.

My original plan was for our gathering to be a one-time event. But at the conclusion of that first meeting, everyone repeated a variation on a word that meant a great deal to me: "Let's do this one more time." *More.* Our time together that second year concluded with the same desire. So we planned a repeat. As groups often do, we thought some kind of name or label would be good, something to call ourselves. We wrestled awhile but couldn't agree on anything. Then one year found us at a Catholic retreat center in Colorado Springs. The nun at the front desk asked the name of our group, and I blurted out, "The Notorious Sinners." She grinned and replied, "And what makes you so notorious?" Her question was rhetorical, but I laughed, and our moniker stuck. The name fit like a hand in a glove. Mike Yaconelli perfectly described the group in his book *Messy Spirituality*:

The Notorious Sinners meet yearly at spiritual-retreat centers, where from the moment we arrive, we find ourselves in trouble with the centers' leadership. We don't act like most contemplatives who come to spiritual-retreat centers—reserved, quiet, silently seeking the voice of God. We're a different kind of contemplative—earthy, bois-terous, noisy, and rowdy, tromping around our souls seeking God, hanging out with a rambunc-tious Jesus who is looking for a good time in our hearts. A number of us smoke cigars, about half are recovering alcoholics, and a couple of the men could embarrass a sailor with their language. Two of the Notorious Sinners show up on their Harleys, complete with leather pants and leather jackets.[16]

The men, minus me, gathered this past August 2010 in Vail, Colorado, marking yet "one more time." So how many years is that now? We can't remember, and we don't care. It's interesting for me to think about this group now. I had spent time in the Marines with other soldiers, time in monasteries among monks, and time among uncloistered brothers serving the poor. The Notorious Sinners are a strange mixture of the best aspects of all those prior experiences.

The format for our time together has changed only a little

over the years. It continues to be a safe place for a group of men to open our hearts to one another, listen, pray, and celebrate Communion. In the best sense of the word—*sanctuary*. In no way do I want to give the impression that every year was some mystical, miracle-heavy experience. There were hard years, times when my alcoholism and an alcoholic's behaviors became the sun around which everything else revolved and sometimes got scorched. I am not proud of those times, but they occurred nonetheless.

The Notorious Sinners: *Back:* Bob Stewart, Alan Hubbard, me, Paul Sheldon, Devlin Donaldson, Fil Anderson, John Krahm, Paul Johnston, John Peter Smith *Front:* Mickey Elfers, Mike Yaconelli

Author Stephen King once said,

Without unvarnished, tough-love truth-telling
from their own kind—the voices that say, "You're
lying about that, Freckles"—the addict has a tendency to fall back into his old ways. And the chief
old way … is lying through one's teeth.[17]

Several of my good friends, men of my own kind, confronted
me over the years about my lying. It wasn't so much the lies about
the big things as the lies about the little stuff, the need to lie at
all. Why does an alcoholic lie about the petty? To stay in practice.
Alcoholism isn't called "the Liar's Disease" for nothing.

Those confrontations never went well. I only wish I could
have trusted then what I believe now. There's not a chance those
confrontations ever came from a place of malice; they were always
rooted in love. However, I always heard their words as criticism,
and as such, I reacted in defensive anger. For me, the anger was
simply a mask, a mask for fear. I dimly suspected that then, but I
can confess it now.

My health has kept me from meeting with the Sinners these last
few years. But I have been encouraged that they have continued to
gather on their own and open their hearts and listen and pray and

celebrate Communion, one more time. They have grown beyond me, a bittersweet reality. A number of the men have visited me lately and told me of the continued faithfulness of the Notorious Sinners. Those stories have brought me sheer joy.

I was deeply moved years ago when reading Robert Johnson's memoir *Balancing Heaven and Earth*. One of the passages I marked heavily with asterisks recounts the contents of a vivid dream Johnson experienced one night. I included that passage in my book *Ruthless Trust*. I believe these words are now a fitting, living tribute to my good friends. Some have criticized that the passage breaks all rules of orthodoxy. It's probably helpful to know that one of the rules of the Sinners has always been "There are no rules."

A prosecutor presented all of the sins of commission and omission that I was responsible for throughout my life, and the list was very long indeed. That went on for hours, and it fell on me like a landslide. I was feeling worse and worse to the point where the soles of my feet were hot. After hours of accusations from the prosecution, a group of angels appeared to conduct my defense. All they could say was, "But he loved." They began chanting this over and over again in a chorus: "But he loved. But he loved. But he loved." This continued until dawn, and in the end the angels won, and I was safe.[18]

Of all the Notorious Sinners, I have known Paul Sheldon the longest. As I've looked back through my journal entries and notes about the people in my life, I have constantly referred to him as "my best friend." However, I do not believe that the word *best* honors my relationship with Paul. I rather prefer the word *oldest*.

Back: Gene Barnes, Paul Johnston, Devlin Donaldson, John Krahm, Alan Hubbard
Front: Fil Anderson, Paul Sheldon, me, Bob Stewart, Butch Farabow

Paul first heard me speak at a cathedral in Mobile, Alabama, in 1972. I was preaching what is known in the Catholic Church as a *novena*—nine days of public or private prayer around a special occasion or intention. It is based on the nine days the disciples and Mary spent in prayer between the Ascension and Pentecost Sunday. I've asked him out of curiosity what it was about my first message that affected him so. His consistent reply has been, "Brennan, I just knew 'that's the truth.'" As others have done over the years, Paul sought out a friendship, something beyond nine days. It wasn't an immediate connection; in fact, it took almost two years for us to become close. But once we did, we were. The booze helped.

I know there is a cadre of young Christian leaders these days who find talking theology over beer to be something exhilarating and edgy, as if combining the two hadn't occurred to anyone before. I believe those young men have historical amnesia. Paul Sheldon and I were doing that when those guys weren't even a thought. Paul and I would get drunk and talk about God for hours and hours. Those times were like Christmas.

Paul was a stockbroker at the time, married to a wonderful woman named Jennie, a consummate Southern cook who learned quickly that I loved to eat. Paul and Jennie welcomed me into their lives like I was family, and I cherished their invitation. After I met Roslyn and she became a part of my life, the four of us would go out together—Paul and Jennie and Roslyn and me. Not everyone was comfortable with the idea of double dating with the priest, so the deliberate approval of Roslyn and me on Paul and Jennie's part was something beyond words. They chose us, unconditionally; it was huge. Whenever I came to Mobile or was close by, we'd all get together, and Jennie would cook a meal I deemed "under the mercy." We'd laugh and talk and joke and bask in the warmth of what is often an uncommon sun—friendship. Those times were like even more Christmas.

The booze always flowed freely between Paul and me. But in November of 1980, Paul stopped drinking. I didn't. Our friendship did not cease on that day, nothing like that, but it did change. In terms of the dynamics of any relationship, if one person changes, the relationship changes; it is not the same as it was. No way it can be. Paul's unchaining himself from the bottle gave him some clarity and perspective that I did not have. I thought I did, but I didn't. In other words, Paul got honest and I did not.

I mentioned earlier that a handful of Notorious Sinners confronted me on various occasions for lying. One of those stalwart souls was Paul. In early 2000, he had noticed I'd made some statements that simply were not true. I tried to brush them off as exaggerations, but Paul called them lies. He had also noticed an anger in my preaching that concerned him; his literal words were "It scared me." My oldest friend shared his concerns with me. Some might immediately pull out the phrase "tough love," but remembering that time now, his were nothing short of tender, heartfelt words. But an alcoholic's best defense is to get defensive, and so I did. Our relationship did not dissolve, but it did splinter somewhat; and it felt fragile for a while after that. Days drift by slowly after a soul wound, and that's how I experienced Paul's confrontation. But if I've learned anything about the world of grace, it's that failure is always a chance for a do-over.

Less than two years later, I made a visit to Paul at his home in Point Clear, Alabama. I was still intent on playing defense, but Paul surprised me with an offensive play that won the match. He told me he wouldn't retract any of his concerns, but despite them, he did not want to lose our friendship. Now, probably those words by themselves would have been enough, but Paul's words were bathed in tears, a man's tears. Most people don't know what to do with a man's tears. I'm still not sure I do. Despite all our efforts at honesty, men are still expected to be strong, competitive, and in control. Tears are, unfortunately, not on the most-wanted list. But there are rare misty-eyed men who in the largesse of God's grace happen to befriend us and reveal to us a different way of living, one fiercely tender and loyal. Such a man is Paul Sheldon, and on that day his tears stanched a wound that I could have let fester for years.

I wish I could also report that his tears stopped the flow of my drinking and exaggeration and anger, but that wouldn't be true. What they did do was heal a friendship that would still suffer but would be stronger than before.

People talk easily of wounded healers, as if they are everywhere walking among us. I don't know about that. I do know that I know one personally. His name is Paul, and he is my oldest friend.

17

Now I want to shift my focus to three people: Frances Brennan; my brother, Rob; and my mother.

Frances was my second mother, so to speak; Rob was and will always be my hero; and my mother was, well, my mother. What's common about all three is the degree of influence they had on my life and the fact that all three have died. I had lost Joey when I was a little boy and then Dominique when I was a Little Brother, but it had been years since death had visited me so closely. I had forgotten just how much it stings.

The little-known Greek word *hetaira* refers to that rare woman who can be a companion to a man—not a sexual partner or wife but a woman who provides a grace and charm highly valued by men. Our current language comes up short in finding a word for this capacity in a woman; modern examples are rare. If pressed for such a word, I would say *Ma*. To me, Ma was Frances Brennan, the perfect hetaira woman to me. Her son Ray was my best friend from the Marines. He died of smoke inhalation in a five-alarm house fire in Chicago, and after his tragic death, I adopted his mother as my second mother. I was not able to visit her as much as I would've liked, but I tried to check in whenever possible.

Ma was the epitome of a feisty Irish woman. On one of my visits with her, I called in a favor through a mutual friend and showed up at her house in a chartered limousine. She stood on the porch and shook her head back and forth. I stepped out and announced, "Get dressed, Ma, we're going to the Ritz-Carlton for lunch." I might as well have told her we were going to the moon, but she got dolled up and off we went. "Ma, you've got to get the shrimp cocktail, its outta this world." I think that menu item was probably around fifteen to twenty dollars in those days, enough for her to protest: "Absolutely not! We can't afford that!" I kept insisting it was my treat; actually it *was* my pleasure, something that brought me great joy. Ma reluctantly agreed, and after the waiter delivered it to our table, she wolfed it down, then leaned over with a grin and asked, "Can we get another one of those?" I think I was as surprised at her question as she was about the limo. I couldn't help but laugh and said, "You bet, Ma!"

"You bet!" became an affirmation between the two of us, a phrase that meant much more than the words themselves. We repeated them to each other often. I believe they were a blessing, much like a priest might say, "The Lord bless and keep you."

There were two Brennan boys: my good friend Ray and his brother, Edward. As a child Edward had experienced some kind of brain injury that left him bound to a stroller at all times. He was not toilet trained or ambulatory and his speech was usually a garbled cry. Mr. and Mrs. Brennan cared for Edward in their home for years, feeding, bathing, changing diapers, and performing the quotidian disciplines one would for an infant. After her husband's death, Ma continued caring for Edward on her own. I know that my visits were a break in the love-filled monotony of her days.

I hold a memory of Ma during the time I was speaking at St. Denis Catholic Church on the west side of Chicago. We were having a five-day meeting starting on Sunday morning and concluding on Thursday evening. Finding a sitter for Edward was difficult, but Ma came to several services, something that meant the world to me. My message on Tuesday was a challenge to be more kind and compassionate and loving to your neighbor.

Later that day, I was visiting with Ma in her home and she said, "Richie [she always called me Richie], I've gotta have more of that kindness toward people. Please pray for me." Just then the telephone rang. Ma answered it and talked into the receiver with cupped hands.

When she hung up the phone, I asked, "Who was that?"

I will never forget her response: "That was my niece; she's such a pain in the ass. See what I mean, Richie, you gotta pray for me!"

"You bet, Ma!"

Mom, Dad, Frances "Ma" Brennan, me, and Geraldine

One evening I had been speaking in Baton Rouge, Louisiana, and returned home to New Orleans exhausted around 10:00 p.m. As I walked in the door, I saw the red light on the answering machine blinking. The recorded voice was soft but tense: "Mrs. Brennan is dying. Her one request is to see you." I couldn't get a flight out that night, so I caught the first to Chicago the next morning. A taxi took me farther into San Pierre, Indiana, to the Little Sisters of Mary nursing home.

Ma had suffered a dizzy spell one day and fell and broke her hip. That day was the end of her in-home care of Edward. It was imperative to find a place for him while she recovered. With the help of some friends, I discovered a nursing facility run by the Little Sisters of Mary. As a gift to all of us, they were gracious enough to take Edward in as well. Edward required almost around-the-clock attention. At the conclusion of her therapy, Ma decided to sell the house she'd known for years and stay with Edward and the Little Sisters for good. If Edward's care was beyond her reach, at least his body could be close by.

I finally arrived at the nursing home around 9:00 p.m. As I entered her room, a nun was sitting beside the bed, praying for my ninety-one-year-old second mother. Ma weighed maybe sixty pounds by that point. "She's been asking for you, waiting for you." Ma didn't just love me; she liked me, enough, I believe, to wait until I arrived to say good-bye. I moved toward her bed, and she pointed to her lips. I sensed her request. I leaned in and kissed Ma on the lips. She whispered, "More." I kissed her a second time, and again she smiled and said, "More."

I kissed my feisty hetaira woman three times, probably to the shock of the nun nearby. I didn't care. I don't know what all a kiss holds, but that night I hoped ours held grace sufficient for the next step in Ma's journey. For the next hour and a half I sat and watched the faint rise and fall of her chest, and then she was finished. I do not believe death gained a victory in that moment; I believe Ma was fully and finally home. But I did feel death's sting on this side of life. I believed I would see Ma again, but until then I had lost a mother and a friend.

I've often wondered about those three kisses in Ma's last moments. I choose to view them much like Jesus' repeated question to Peter—"Do you love me?" If that's what Ma Brennan was asking, then I trust my lips provided the answer—"You bet, Ma!"

Edward didn't live long after Ma died. Her voice was no longer in his room but rather in another place, another reality. I believe Edward just followed her voice home.

I mentioned that I changed my name when I was ordained with the Franciscans. The brothers thought I chose Brennan after Saint Brennan, a somewhat-obscure Irish saint. In some sense that's true. But more so, the name I chose is a sign of how much I loved that scrappy Irish woman and her two sons.

I had a dream where Ma is standing before Saint Peter, wondering if she'll get through the pearly gates. Saint Peter steps to the side and says, "Come on in, Frances." She just stands there in disbelief, kind of like the day I showed up in the limo, and says, "Really, I can come in?" Jesus steps around

Saint Peter and gives her a big bear hug and says, "You bet, Ma!" That's a good dream.

Frances Brennan's death was a blow for me. Another such blow came in 1990 when death took my brother, Rob. Rob eventually became a cop and I became a priest. My father often said, "I have one son to keep me outta jail and one son to keep me outta hell."

Rob worked in one of New York's precincts, known there as he was known in our neighborhood—for being tuff. He was decorated countless times for gallantry in action. I was invited once to speak at the precinct's annual Communion breakfast. I waxed eloquent about all the ways those men selflessly served the people in our community, emphasizing their redemption of the word *pig*—pride, integrity, guts. I have to admit, I thought my speech was brilliant. After I finished, Ralphie Coen, captain of the precinct, stood up, looked at my brother a moment, then stared at me and shook his head. "My God, not from the same womb." Ralphie obviously knew a dreamer with soft hands when he saw one.

But my brother ran into something tuffer than him—cancer.

My mother had at first refused to visit Rob in the hospital. I'm not entirely sure why; she just wouldn't go see him. I was summoned from New Orleans to Rob's bedside and dropped what I was doing and left.

I stopped by my mother's house and informed her, "I'm not asking. We're going to see Rob tomorrow." All I got was an "Oh, all right."

We went to the hospital, and my mother, who had walked with ease from the house to the car and from the car to the hospital door, suddenly needed a wheelchair. I wheeled her into Rob's room, and she began telling him all of her woes. Rob looked at his wife, Celie, then at our mother and me and said, "Get her outta here." I had grown to love Celie as much as I loved Rob. She looked me in the eyes, and I could interpret her request: "Please, Brennan, do as Rob asked." So I took my mother and we left. I drove her home, and my brother died two days later, August 8, 1990.

My parents had loaned him four thousand dollars for the down payment on a house. As I drove my parents to Robert's wake, my mother whined, "Well, Emmett, I guess we can kiss that four thousand dollars good-bye."

I turned around and screamed, "That's enough, Mom!"

We drove the rest of the way in silence. One of Rob's fellow officers approached me at the wake. "Your brother was the most fearless man I ever met. My wife would be a widow and my kids would be orphans if not for your brother. He was a true hero." I said, "Yes, he was mine too." As we grew up, I adored Rob because he was my older brother. Rob did everything before I did; he was born first, left the house first, went to Korea first, got married first, had a career first. But I never thought he would die first.

Rob and me on confirmation day

I was there for the funeral of Frances Brennan, as I was for Rob's. But I missed another that was very important.

Before I tell that story, I want to share something with you. It is a list from a journal I kept during another alcohol-rehab treatment following my divorce from Roslyn. Each item on the list is a self-description. I wrote the list in an attempt to once more get honest about my condition. I believe the items reveal the kind of man who would miss his own mother's funeral.

1. Being smug, superior, arrogant. I constantly name-dropped—Burl Ives, Amy Grant, Mike Ditka. I hated this trait in other people but saw nothing wrong with it in my life.

2. Blaming/accusing. I blamed Roslyn (after the divorce) for insensitivity; she placed the care of her two daughters and the upkeep of our home above me—how dare she?

3. Defiance. When Roslyn remarked that my relapses were becoming more frequent, I flatly and loudly refused.

4. Evading/dodging. When close friends raised the issue of my alcoholism, I changed the subject.

5. Intellectualizing. I was constantly trying to think myself into a new way of living instead of loving myself into a new way of thinking (see, I just did it again).

6. Judging/moralizing. I often passed judgment on the rigidity and stupidity of the pope, the bishops, and the church for not permitting a married priesthood. I also loathed my critics.

7. Justifying. "Look, anyone who has worked as hard as I have, carrying a superhuman schedule, is entitled ..."

8. Joking. I used self-deprecating humor to give the impression that I am humble and don't take myself seriously.

9. Lying. Quite possibly an umbrella word for all of the above.

10. Rationalization. I claimed burnout and refused the relentless claims of needy people, including members of my family.

That last item factors into the most shameful episode of my life. I wrote out the following almost like a fiction story. I only wish it were fiction, but it's not. You don't always get what you ask for.

The phone rings and you're given a choice—answer it or not. Maybe I shouldn't have. Maybe I should have sidestepped it like a land mine. But I answered it. It turned out to be a foghorn of bad news.

The voice on the other end belonged to someone I loved. My sister spoke two words: "Mom died." It was February 1993.

After we hung up, I was aware of nothing but a single emotion. I could tell you that I felt sadness or regret or even fear, but I've vowed to be ruthlessly honest with myself in these pages. After Gerry called, all I thought was *God, what a bother.* I packed a bag and booked the flight.

I was living in New Orleans at the time. My sister lived in Belmar, New Jersey. My mother had been in an Alzheimer's facility for two years not far from where Gerry lived. My mother had completely lost her memory. But I hadn't. And my past with her created a core of pain in myself that I'd wrestled with most of my life.

I flew into Newark and took a cab to Belmar. I stayed in a motel near the church where the funeral was to be held.

I stopped at a liquor store before checking in and bought a quart of their cheapest Scotch. While others arranged flowers and pressed their shirts, I locked the door of my room, pulled the curtains, and drank. I wanted to forget, but unfortunately the Scotch only slowed the approach of my memories. Eventually thoughts of my mother broke through—the tone of her voice, her sayings, and mostly, the shame. Like a good alcoholic, I kept drinking and drinking and drinking. I thought it was my only defense. Eventually, everything faded a shade deeper than black.

"Ashes to ashes, dust to dust." Surely the priest spoke those words over the casket of my mother, Amy Manning, but I cannot be certain because I missed my mother's funeral. I was back at the motel waking up from a blackout, trying to remember where I was.

The fact was that I was in a motel room in Belmar, New Jersey. But the truth was that I was in some distant place, having squandered my mother's last respects with drunkenness. In that moment I felt the most profound shame of my life. *My God, what kind of a man am I? How could that have happened?*

I didn't visit my mother's gravesite later that day either. The reality is I've never visited it.

I've been asked a certain question countless times over the course of my ministry. Sometimes it has been asked with genuine sincerity; other times I'm sure it was a loaded pharisaical grenade: "Brennan, how could you relapse into alcoholism after your Abba encounters?" Here is the response I gave in *The Ragamuffin Gospel* in 1990:

> It is possible because I got battered and bruised by loneliness and failure; because I got discouraged, uncertain, guilt-ridden, and took my eyes off Jesus. Because the Christ-encounter did not transfigure me into an angel. Because justification

by grace through faith means I have been set in
a right relationship with God, not made the
equivalent of a patient etherized on a table.[19]

Twenty-one years later I stand by what I wrote; those words
are as true for me now as they were then and on the day of my
mother's funeral. That paragraph from *Ragamuffin Gospel* spoke
to many people; they've told me so time after time. I must admit
though that from where I sit today the paragraph is a bit much, a
little wordy. I believe I can now whittle the lines down to a three-
word response that incorporates all the truth of a verbose 1990s
ragamuffin into a 2011 ragamuffin's preference for brevity.

Question: "Brennan, how could you relapse into
alcoholism after your Abba encounters?"
Answer: "These things happen."

I'd like to give my good friend Fil Anderson the final word
in this section. These words come from Fil's latest book *Breaking
the Rules*. He knows all about the response "These things happen."

My highest hope is for all of us to stop trying to
fool others by appearing to have our act together.
As people living in intimate union with God, we
need to become better known for what and who

we actually are. Perhaps a good place to begin would be telling the world—before the world does its own investigation—that we're not as bad as they think. We're worse. At least I know that I'm worse.

Let's get real. For every mean-spirited, judgmental thing some preacher has said, I've thought something nastier, more hateful and more cutting about one of my neighbors. For every alleged act of homophobia by my fellow Christians, I've done something stupid to demonstrate my manliness. For every brother or sister whose moral failure has been exposed, I've failed privately. No matter how boring followers of Jesus may appear to be to the outsiders, they don't know the half of it; trust me.... If we really believe the gospel we proclaim, we'll be honest about our own beauty and brokenness, and the beautiful broken One will make himself known to our neighbors through the chinks in our armor—and in theirs.[20]

Part III

ME

18

I celebrated my seventy-seventh birthday in April. If you asked me whether what I have done in my life defines my life, I would answer, "No." That's not to diminish my sins or humble-bumble my successes. It is simply to affirm a grace often realized only in the winter of life. The winter is stark but also comforting. I am, and have always been, more than the sum of my deeds. Thank God.

If asked whether I have fulfilled my calling as an evangelist, I would answer, "No." That answer is not guilt-ridden or shame-faced. It is to witness to a larger truth, again more clearly seen in my later days. My calling is, and always has been, to a life filled with family and friends and alcohol and Jesus and Roslyn and notoriously good sinners.

If asked whether I am going gently into old age, I would answer, "No." That's just plain honest. It is true that when you are old, you are often led where you would rather not go. In a wisdom that some days I admit feels foolish, God has ordained the later days of our lives to look shockingly similar to that of our earliest: as dependent children.

If asked whether I am finally letting God love me, just as I am, I would answer, "No, but I'm trying."

Belmar, New Jersey, has been called "the Irish Riviera." Wealthy New Yorkers used to drive the hour down the coast and renew themselves in the sand and surf. It was a resort, a summer place. But all that has changed. Now the cottages and boardwalk are occupied year-round; Belmar and its environs are full of residents. I am one of them. My apartment sits back off the street, behind a lovely old home with a porch and sycamore trees. My residence is almost hidden. In a very real sense these days, so am I.

I tried for a short time to resume my speaking ministry in 2008. This was attempted with the help of my good friend Fil Anderson. Fil was pure support and encouragement at a time when I needed it dearly. We would share the speaking responsibilities on a given weekend, me leaning on Fil more than the other way around. As has been the case for more than forty years, if I am not traveling and speaking, I don't know what to do with myself, so I had to try. I suffered two falls prior to that brief try-again period—one figurative and the other literal. These falls pressed my cospeaking engagements with Fil into another realm entirely, one where a tried-and-true friend is most recognizable.

In March 2009, I stood before a packed church in Charlotte, North Carolina, ready to greet those gathered with my signature opening, followed by some Yiddish humor, like I've done a thousand times before:

In the words of Francis of Assisi as he met Brother Dominique on the road to Umbria, *Hi* …

One day Alan the tailor was walking down the street, and he meets Moisha the banker and asks where he's going.

"Synagogue," Moisha says, looking horribly distraught.

"Why?"

"I've gotta talk to the rabbi."

"Why you've gotta talk to the rabbi?" Alan asks.

"Aye," says Moisha, "A terrible thing has happened! My son become a Christian."

"Oh, Moisha," says Alan, "Let me tell you a very funny thing. *My* son is a Christian!"

The two of them arrive at the synagogue and open the door. Out comes the rabbi, who says, "Moisha, Alan, what is going on?"

Alan says, "We got a catastrophe in our families. Our two sons become Christians."

"Into my office!" says the rabbi. "Lock the door."

After a long pause he looks up and says, "Let me tell you a very funny thing. *My* son is a Christian."

"No!" says Alan.

"We are lost!" says Moisha. "What are we going to do, rabbi? You the Answer Man!"

"Yes, we do something," says the rabbi. "Come with me."

So they march across the synagogue and into the sanctuary.

The rabbi says, "Kneel. Shut up. I pray. Yahweh, God of Abraham, God of Isaac, God of Jacob, God of Israel, God of the prophets, what on earth is going on? Judaism is gone down the tube. Everyone's becoming a Christian! Yahweh, give us a word. Yahweh, speak a voice to us."

Long pause. Finally God says, "But let me tell you a very funny thing …"

I *should* have been able to do that bit, but shortly into my opening, my mind went blank. For someone who has preached for years the motto of my friend Mary Michael O'Shaughnessy— "Today I will not should on myself"—that was an evening I wish I could have. I should've been able to do that bit, but I couldn't. I just stood there trying, desperately trying, but I had nothing. I simply could not remember my lines. That had never happened before. I looked out at the crowd and asked them to please pray for me.

But let me tell you a very funny thing. After a long, awkward pause, the crowd surprised me; they gave me a standing ovation. I was being affirmed for my silence. That had also never happened before. I don't know when I've felt such genuine compassion from a group of people. I retired to my room and got some rest. The next day I was back hitting my marks, able to conduct the scheduled sessions as if nothing had happened. But something had happened. I have no idea what the people gathered there in Charlotte thought about that dark Friday night. I'm not even entirely sure what I thought about it, other than it scared me.

Following that weekend, my return home was nothing short of traumatic. Because of significant problems with my vision, I fell down an escalator at the New Orleans airport, breaking my shoulder and ribs. That crushing pain, on the heels of my dark Friday, told me that Brennan Manning, like Belmar, was no longer a summer place.

I have said countless times that losing our illusions is difficult because illusions are the stuff we live by. We believe we're invincible until cancer comes knocking, or we believe we're making a comeback until we tumble down the stairs. God strips away those falsehoods because it is better to live naked in truth than clothed in fantasy. The last few years have been a "stripping away" like I've never experienced. About all I'm left with now is rags, somewhat fitting I guess for a man who has preached such a gospel. If I ever was a ragamuffin, I am now. For ragamuffins, God's name is Mercy; or in the present vernacular of my life—*Help*.

Nowadays if I want to put on my jeans and shirt, someone has to help me. If I want to eat a slice of pepperoni pizza from Pete & Elda's or an ice-cream cone, someone has to help me. If I have to go to the bathroom, I need help. To turn up the volume on the Yankees game, I need help. To access my medicine or open my Diet Coke, I must have help. To get into bed at night, help. To rise in the morning, help. To nap in the afternoon, help. To write this book, help. Carlo Carretto wrote, "We are what we pray." These are days of prayer without ceasing—"Help me! Have mercy on me!" And my Father, who is so very fond of me, does.

In addition to my sister, Gerry, and her husband, Art, there is a man who has been my helper, the person who does all these things, since I returned to Belmar in 2009. Is this the way I've wanted things to be? No, definitely not. If I had my druthers, I would still be in New Orleans along the great big Muddy and among my friends in Algiers.

My caregiver's name is Richard. We listen to CNN every
day and the Yankees or the Knicks, depending on the season. He
cooks a mean hot dog and keeps the water or Diet Coke nearby.
He locks up at night and opens up in the morning. I've stumbled
and fallen a few times in my house, and he's always picked me up
and dusted me off, much like a parent would do. He gets me to my
appointments on time. He has been someone to watch over me.
I find myself now back in the general vicinity of my childhood.
I am being cared for in a way I longed for as a child. And of all
the people I could spend my days in the company of, I have been
befriended by a man with my very own given name.

And accompanied by my friend Richard, I have a lot of
time on my hands these days; time to think, maybe like I haven't
in a long while. So I'm going to give you "the last sermon you'll
ever need." If it sounds like there are traces in it of sermons I've
preached before, that's because there are.

19

Scripture is full of ragamuffins. I've overlooked one, no doubt for the obvious reason that he doesn't appear to be a ragamuffin at first sight. His exploits are heroic, the stuff of legend. But stretching my mind to look deeper, I've seen his rags. His name was Samson, the long-haired strong man who took Nazirite vows, the last and most famous of the Old Testament judges, the warrior who slew the lion with his bare hands and a thousand Philistines with the jawbone of an ass. But his storied life ended in a prison, his hair shaved, his eyes gouged out, weak, blind, dependent, little more than a child. In one final mockery, Samson was chained between twin temple pillars at the feast of the god Dagon for the amusement of the people. But not everything was as it appeared. Had the Philistines assembled on that day looked closer, they would have noticed a lengthening shadow on the ragamuffin's head; his hair had begun to grow back and therefore his strength. In one final witness to the God of Israel, Samson seized the chains and pulled. He brought the house down, literally.

With what strength I have left, I want to grab the chains and pull, one last time. My hope, as always, is to point to the God too good to be true, my Abba. I've no delusions of heroically bringing down the house of fear that imprisons so many. My desire is to witness, nothing else. My message, unchanged for more than fifty years, is this: *God loves you unconditionally, as you are and not as you should be, because nobody is as they should be.* It is the message of grace, the life-shattering gift my heart experienced in February 1956. It is the life-sustaining gift I remain broken by now in February 2011.

Some have labeled my message one of "cheap grace." In my younger days, their accusations were a gauntlet thrown down, a challenge. But I'm an old man now and I don't care. My friend Mike Yaconelli used the phrase *unfair grace*, and I like that, but I have come across another I would like to leave you with. I believe Mike would like it; I know I do. I found it in the writings of the Episcopal priest Robert Farrar Capon. He calls it *vulgar grace.*

In Jesus, God has put up a "Gone Fishing" sign
on the religion shop. He has done the whole job

in Jesus once and for all and simply invited us to believe it—to trust the bizarre, unprovable proposition that in him, every last person on earth is already home free without a single religious exertion: no fasting till your knees fold, no prayers you have to get right or else, no standing on your head with your right thumb in your left ear and reciting the correct creed—no nothing.... The entire show has been set to rights in the Mystery of Christ—even though nobody can see a single improvement. Yes, it's crazy. And yes, it's wild, and outrageous, and *vulgar*. And any God who would do such a thing is a God who has no taste. And worst of all, it doesn't sell worth beans. But it is Good News—the only permanently good news there is—and therefore I find it absolutely captivating.[21] (italics mine)

My life is a witness to vulgar grace—a grace that amazes as it offends. A grace that pays the eager beaver who works all day long the same wages as the grinning drunk who shows up at ten till five. A grace that hikes up the robe and runs breakneck toward the prodigal reeking of sin and wraps him up and decides to throw a party no *ifs*, *ands*, or *buts*. A grace that raises bloodshot eyes to a dying thief's request—"Please, remember me"—and assures him, "You bet!" A grace that is the pleasure of the Father, fleshed out in the carpenter Messiah, Jesus the Christ, who left His Father's side not for heaven's sake but for our sakes, yours and mine. This vulgar grace is indiscriminate compassion. It works without asking anything of us. It's not cheap. It's free, and as such will always be a banana peel for the orthodox foot and a fairy tale for the grown-up sensibility. Grace is sufficient even though we huff and puff with all our might to try to find something or someone it cannot cover. Grace is enough. He is enough. Jesus is enough.

John, the disciple Jesus loved, ended his first letter with this line: "Children, be on your guard against false gods." In other words, steer clear of any god you can comprehend. Abba's love cannot be comprehended. I'll say it again: Abba's love cannot be comprehended.

20

One of the questions I've often asked myself is, What makes a man drown himself in drink to the point that he passes out and misses his own mother's funeral?

It has seemed like a huge question to me, but eventually I realized: It is not *the* question. There is another question behind it, a more seminal one that forms and informs all my others. Not long ago, I came across a small yellowed piece of paper in my stack of writings. It has the letterhead "Willie Juan Ministries" with a scratch below it from my own hand, a single line, a question:

"What is the telltale sign of a trusting heart?"

I cannot remember when I wrote it or what might have prompted the question. Yet it is there, evidence of a ragamuffin's lifelong wondering. Here is my answer, the answer that is, as Thomas Merton wrote, "the 'Yes' which brings Christ into the world."

A trusting heart is forgiven and, in turn, forgives.

I know that's true because of an experience I had on a November day in 2003. My mother had been dead and gone for close to ten years. As I was praying about other things, her face flashed across the window of my mind. It was not a worn face like that of an old mother or grandmother, but a child's face. I saw my mother as a little six-year-old girl kneeling on the windowsill of the orphanage in Montreal. Her nose was pressed against the glass; she was begging God to send her a mommy and daddy who would whisk her away and love her without condition. As I looked, I believe I finally *saw* my mother; she was a ragamuffin too. And all my resentment and anger fell away.

The little girl turned and walked toward me. As she drew closer, the years flew by and she stood before me an aged woman. She said, "You know, I messed up a lot when you were a kid. But you turned out okay." Then my old mother did something she'd never done before in her life, never once. She kissed me on the lips and on both cheeks. At that moment I knew that the hurt between my mother and me was real and did matter, but that it was okay. The trusting heart gives a second chance; it is forgiven and, in turn, forgives. I looked at my mother and said, "I forgive you." She smiled and said, "I guess sometimes you do get what you ask for."

Dad, Mom, and me

A WORD AFTER

I stepped into the path of Brennan Manning late in his life. Those I have talked with who knew him in his prime have consistently said, "I wish you'd have known him then." I wish that too. But I didn't, and maybe if I had, my assistance on his memoir would have been biased or skewed. It's hard to know. I do wish I'd known him then.

His brother-in-law, Art Rubino, told me, "If I had a dollar for every life he's touched, we'd all be sunning in Acapulco." Art's right. The overwhelming testimony to his ministry is best summed up in that evening when he stood before a crowd and could not remember what to say. The people stood and applauded the man whose patchwork pants and ragamuffin life had become exterior symbols of the inward gift, the grace greater than the sum of his sins and their own. Yet that evening also represents the "glass darkly," for while Brennan preached and taught of God's furious longing for us and the joy that comes from the Abba experience, that message often seemed elusive to his own grasp. I have no doubt there were bright mornings and luminous afternoons for Brennan, but there have also been many, many dark nights. I suppose the preacher always preaches the message he needs most. I believe that is true of my friend Brennan. That his message has been the one we needed most too is something extra. Or to use one of Brennan's favorite Cajun words, *lagniappe*—compliments of the house. Grace.

The older you get, the more you sense that much of life is about timing. I have mentioned that word to many influenced by Brennan's life, proposing that his message came along at the right time, the *kairos*. They have all immediately nodded, as if that was something they'd felt but not verbalized. In that regard, Brennan has played a role much like a midwife, helping Christ be born in us today or back when you first read *Abba's Child* or during that life-changing Young Life retreat. His consistent banging on the drums of God's unconditional love sounded at a time when many of us had about "had it up to here" with religion and church and, probably most importantly, ourselves. We were the tired, poor, self-hating huddled masses yearning to be free, and along came a patchwork preacher who grinned and said, "You already are. Abba loves you. Let's go get some chocolate ice cream."

Brennan loved to read, and as such, filled his books and talks with stories he'd found along the way, stories that always gave texture to the invasion of grace in our world. And in that spirit, I'd like to share with you a scene from Kent Meyers' novel *Twisted Tree*; and although he has never read the novel, I believe it honors the essence of Brennan Manning.

The scene finds Caleb coming upon an accident, a car lying upside down in barbed wire. Three patrolmen are standing near the car; someone is lying between them beneath a tarp. Caleb is tempted not to stop, but does. Caleb used to be a priest before he fell in love with a woman and lost his collar. Now he is just a rancher.

A Native American woman was thrown from the car, not wearing a seat belt. One patrolman says an ambulance will arrive soon, so Caleb turns to go because there is nothing more he can do. As he turns to walk away, he hears one of the men whisper, "He used to be a priest." And then the scene changes; the atmosphere quickens as a different voice raises, the woman's: "A priest?" The injured demands a chance to confess. Caleb tries to redirect her focus, but she is insistent. The scene continues:

> "Once a priest, always a priest.... It is indelible," she said.
>
> I assumed I knew what she meant: how the soul is marked by sacraments, and nothing can

erase the mark, no omission or commission, no thought or word or deed, and the power I'd been given remained, regardless of belief....

I hadn't felt holy for over twenty years, and I knew too well the old lessons of sacred objects that required, for their touching, consecrated hands.... But I'd told myself—I had to—that grace cannot be weakened by anything a human being does or disbelieves. It runs on, a pure thing, in spite of, as well as because of, us.

Caleb bows his head and they begin the old familiar words. The broken woman offers up the things she needs to say, and then the broken priest gives order to her suffering by assigning a penance. Caleb finishes by forgiving and blessing her.

"*Pilamaya*," she said when I finished.[22]

That final italicized word, *pilamaya*, is Lakota. It means "thank you."

Brennan has never stopped doggedly reminding us of our deepest longing—that grace, God's unconditional love for us, runs on, pure, in spite of, as well as because of, us. He has been a priest among us, giving indelible order to our suffering. Once a priest, always a priest. But he has also been broken among us, time after time, forgiven and blessed, as we all are.

    Thank you, Brennan.

John Blase

Now there's no more crowds and no more lights,
still all is grace.
Now my eyes are wrapped in endless night,
still all is grace.
Now I pace the dark and sleep the day
yet I still can hear my Father say—
"all is grace."

It was easy as a younger man
To squander in the far off land
Where sin was sin, like black is black.
But older brother sin is white,
this doubt that creeps me up at night—
"does Jesus love me still?"

Now I take my meds and hear the game,
still all is grace.
Now old friends drop in and bless my name,
still all is grace.
Now a prodigal I'll always be
yet still my Father runs to me.
All is grace.

PHOTO GALLERY

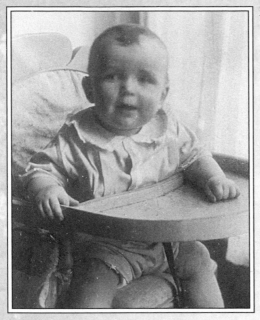

Me (5 months)

Mom, me (3), and Rob (4)

Me (4)

Rob (15), Gerry (5), and me (14)

Rob (*back left*) and me (*front middle*) in a lake in Canada where we spent many summers with family and friends

Mom and Dad

Grandma Anna Manning
(*middle*) with husband,
William (*right*), and
cousin (*left*)

Dad, me, and Mom near the seminary in Loretto, Pennsylvania

Me and Gerry

Mom, me, and Dad

Me with my nieces Katie and
Mary at Christmastime

Me officiating Gerry
and Art's wedding

Dad, Mom, and me
at Christmastime

Me and Roslyn with
Dr. Francis MacNutt

Roslyn and me on
our wedding day

Me and Roslyn

A birthday celebration

The first Notorious Sinners gathering

Notorious Sinners: Gene Barnes, Alan Hubbard, John Peter Smith, Devlin Donaldson, and me

Notorious Sinners: Lou Bauer, Paul Sheldon, John Eames, Alan Hubbard, Mickey Elfers, Paul Johnston, Butch Farabow, me, Bob Stewart, Ed Moise

Preparing
Communion
at a Notorious
Sinners gathering

Art (brother-in-law), Gerry, and me

Having ice cream with my
agent, Rick Christian

LETTERS

I (John) was privileged to sit with the Notorious Sinners in August 2010 in Vail, Colorado. Brennan was not physically present at their gathering, but his spirit was definitely there. I immediately liked these men of different ages and backgrounds. They radiated something I believe they've learned well over the years—grace. I invited each of them to send me a "Dear Brennan" letter for this book. When they asked what the parameters were for the letter, I said, "There are no rules." They seemed to really like that.

*And remember, my sentimental friend, that a heart is not judged
by how much you love, but by how much you are loved by others.*

L. Frank Baum

Dear Brennan,

We first met in Kenya when you came to be the spiritual director for a conference I was the director of called the Christian Medical Dental Society Continuing Medical Education program (CMDS-CME). It was, and still is, a program bringing CME credits to missionary doctors and dentists. I had heard some of your tapes and was fascinated to meet you. Being program director and having control over such things, I placed you in a room next to mine at Brackenhurst Baptist Conference Centre, about an hour outside of Nairobi. I remember being struck that you were frightened about coming to Africa and that after knowing each other only a day you were comfortable sharing that with me.

The missionaries were from all denominations and sponsoring home boards, but, not surprisingly, the largest single group was here with the International Mission Board. Some of our CMDS board members had objected to a renegade, married Franciscan coming to lead a group that had only a handful of Catholic missionaries. But the missionaries clung to your ragamuffin message like refugees around a water truck. With your mixture of profound truth and poetic license, hungry shepherds were fed and healers were themselves healed. It was truly amazing. When you weren't leading the evening worship services, you were being pursued by a steady stream of missionaries who pleaded for individual time with you. You invited the three or four Catholics and myself to celebrate the Eucharist with you in the predawn time before breakfast. I remember being struck by the fact that you had brought with you a large candle, which took up a good portion of the small single piece of luggage you'd brought to Africa. In the light of that candle, in the blending of our voices in ancient ritual prayers, I came to a whole new level of intimacy with our Lord and felt that the Reformers would have done well to have held on to this approach to the sacrament.

Soon after we were all home from Africa, I drove from Louisville to Cincinnati to have dinner with you at the end of a retreat weekend there. During that dinner you wondered what I, as a psychiatrist interested in group dynamics, thought of the idea of getting together a group of Christian men, maybe ten to fourteen, for a week of sharing and praying for one another. Different from the other weekend prayer retreats you led, this would be comprised of men who for the most part knew only you. We'd meet each other at the weekend. You'd pick the participants from men met in your travels; I thought it was just crazy enough to be worth trying. I agreed to assist in any way I could. Out of that evening grew your invitations to all of the others for what would be our first meeting in Gulf Shores. As you know, that was really supposed to be the one and only meeting of the group. But, at the end of it, we all wanted to do it one more time the next year. And it went from there.

Yours,
Bob

Brennan,

We miss you and love you. You know how God has used you in our lives both through your writing and our personal relationship. We want you to know that we are with you in this stage of your life and will continue to pray for you. Your guidance has molded our entire perception of God and His attitude toward us. Seeing God as our Abba would not have been possible had you not been a part of our lives and modeled that concept. We also learned to listen to the "still, small voice" through the disciplines we first heard from you, and that is why we are in the good place we are today.

Thanks and God Bless,
Butch and Suzie

Dear Brennan,

Each day I pray that God will go easy on you. But I thank God that He has you in a safe place with loving caretakers. When I think of the near-miraculous help that you have been to Lolly and me, I am swept away with gratitude. There is no denying that had you not been kicked out of that Catholic venue in Providence and then made your way to our house, my darling Lolly would never have reached recovery from her alcoholism! And can you ever forget celebrating Mass at our house after she returned to treatment and your consecrating thirty tiny pieces of bagel for her to have Holy Communion in her room? And the miracle that God performed when the leftover bagel in my bread box became filled with green mold—but *none of Lolly's thirty pieces were affected!* You figure it out! As you know, Lolly had been drinking to excess for over twenty-five years, had been in several rehab places during that time, and seemed destined to die of the disease. But this visit of yours and her willingness to try again resulted in her sobriety for the next twenty-five years—years of heaven for both of us and our children!

You have made no secret of your struggles with "the creature"! I have told you, and I believe it is true, that the Devil made you a special target and used booze as his weapon! The Devil is frightened of you, Brother Brennan! Have you ever pondered what you could have been or accomplished without booze? As it is and was, you, as a wounded healer, helped bring hundreds of thousands of us sinners to Christ with your simple mantra: "God loves us just as we are—not as we should be."

My wife, Lolly, and I were at a breaking point. I did not
think I could continue to stay married to someone who was so
self-destructive! But I wanted to consult you before moving out
or calling a lawyer. When I did call you, Roslyn said that you
were en route to Providence, Rhode Island, for a week of renewal
at a Catholic church there. Ros also said that you had a layover in
Newark to change planes. So I immediately drove to the Newark
airport and, believe it or not, found you in the midst of that huge
airport! I told you what was going on, and you said that I, under
the circumstances, could leave Lolly—after twenty-five years of
alcoholic drinking! So I drove back to our house in Manhasset,
New York. When I arrived there some three hours later, I found
Lolly all cleaned up and as sober as I had seen her in a long time.
She announced to me that you were coming for dinner! What
had happened was some conservative Catholics at the church you
went to visit in Providence found out that you were married and
reported it to the bishop. The bishop then forbade that parish to
have you speak there, so what did you do? You called Lolly and
said you'd like to come to dinner! So I had to turn around and
pick you up at LaGuardia and home we came. Lolly could not
have been a more willing or welcoming hostess. She loved you,
Brennan. After dinner I retired, and you and Lolly sat up and
talked almost all night! She had sworn that she would never go
back into treatment again, so you can imagine my surprise when,
the next morning (Sunday), you told me that Lolly agreed to go
back to Brunswick Hospital Rehab! You also asked if I had any
Valium in the house, because she could go into convulsions if she

did not have a tranquilizer. I told you that I had nothing like it
in the house and I surely could not find a doctor to prescribe it
on a Sunday! But I went down to our local drugstore, which was
owned by a friend (who also was very aware of Lolly's history—
active alcoholics are pretty public), and he gave me three Valium
pills without a prescription (he could have lost his license!). Lolly
took the pills and we drove out to Brunswick Hospital, about
twenty miles east of us on Long Island and a place she had been
twice before.

You decided to stay with me in Manhasset for a couple
of days. Every morning you would celebrate Mass in my living
room. I had only fresh bagels to use as hosts. I would slice a thin
layer off a bagel, and you would consecrate it and some grape
juice for the body and blood of Christ! I said, "Brennan, would it
be sacrilegious to have you consecrate thirty little pieces of bagel
that I can put in my pyx and take to Lolly? I know she'd like that
and she could have Holy Communion every day of the thirty
days she's scheduled to stay at Brunswick."

You said, "Great idea! That's what the early Christians used
to do—take Eucharist to each others' homes!" Needless to say,
Lolly was delighted to get this sacred gift, and she kept the pyx
in her dresser drawer and consumed one consecrated piece of
bagel every day. You left a couple of days later. So one morning I
went to our bread box where I kept the leftover bagel to have it
for breakfast. I was stunned to discover that it was covered with
mold! I had forgotten that these bagels had no preservatives and
should have been kept in the fridge! I went out to see Lolly that

night and sadly reported what happened to the "mother" bagel. She said, "There is not a sign of mold in the pyx and the little pieces are even still moist!" I was dumbfounded! And they stayed that way for the entire time she was at Brunswick. Brennan, I don't know how you explain this phenomenon, but I call it a miracle. The rest of the story is even more miraculous. As you know, Lolly stayed sober in AA for the rest of her life—over twenty-five years! She passed away September 27, 2009. And the gift of her longtime sobriety was something that my children and I found as close to heaven as I suspect we'll see this side of the grave.

May He continue to bless you and use you!

Love,
John Peter

Brennan,

     I heard two of your boxed sets of tapes before I was blessed
to see you preach at a retreat on Long Island back in the early
eighties. Hearing you in person that Friday night in Manhasset
spun my world around with all of the healing words of Jesus' love
cascading upon me and bringing back all the hours of healing
from the tapes. We celebrated Mass in the early morning hours
the next day in a way I believed Jesus did in the upper room with
the apostles. You later came to preach a weekend retreat at my
parish and stayed at my house. We couldn't advertise the retreat
as we were afraid the bishop would not allow you to be there
since you had gotten married. You reassured me that if only one
person showed up, the Lord meant for that person to be there
and would take care of the details. Word of mouth tripled the
numbers each night!

     My times shared with you in the years that followed were
treasures: going out for ice cream during retreats, staying in
touch during difficult years in our marriages. The incredible gift
of being invited to the gathering of the Sinners was the greatest
gift of lasting deep friendships with your friends from across
the country. The love, honest sharing, and tremendous laughter
we've shared for the past seventeen annual meetings has been a
great blessing. In your wisdom, you had me share a room with
a brother who was going through tough times in his marriage.
Years later I met my wife, Julia, through my relationship with
him and his new wife. You have often joked that my meeting
Julia was one of the greatest gifts of our group. Each day that

I share with her and our two beautiful children, I think of the many blessed relationships that were formed through my relationship with you.

I love you,
John

Brennan,

As the years creep along (twenty since we met), I find myself reflecting more and more on the poignant moments of life, those experiences that sneak up on you and suddenly change everything. As you recall, our friendship was one of those moments that happened based on two unusual phone calls. A friend and I had spent the day together, and when he left, he handed me a tape, saying, "You should listen to this. It's a game changer." Days later I started listening to a talk you gave titled "Pioneers and Settlers" based on a book by Wes Seeliger. Now, I had no idea who Brennan Manning was, but the concept of God as a trail boss who carried a gun and drank straight whiskey was something that had my attention. So much so that when you mentioned your home in New Orleans, I called information, got your home number, and called you to introduce myself. I had to know more about this God you described and the man behind the gravelly voice with a hint of Irish lilt in it. You said, "I'll be out in Oregon next month and need a ride from the airport to my speaking engagement. Let's talk then."

Four years and several shuttles to and from the Portland airport later, I was the one getting the surprise phone call. After brief pleasantries you said, "Hey, Mick, I'm getting my closest friends together for a weekend in August and I'd like you to be there." A simple invitation that led to a lifelong commitment to the Notorious Sinners.

Since then, you and I have buried friends, listened to confessions, laughed and cried on each other's shoulders, and walked

the peaks and valleys together. Hardly simple, always messy, but
never boring. Now as the Sinners get ready to meet again this
year, I am reminded about how two simple phone calls, brief
conversations, a sense of humor, and brutal honesty can bind
people together for life.

I love you, my friend. Keep listening for the phone. I hope
it never stops ringing.

Mick

Dear Brennan,

Nearly three decades have come and gone since our paths
first crossed. Back then the appearance of my life and yours
was pretty darn good. I was a regional director of Young Life in
the Carolinas, frantically living *for* God rather than *with* God.
My cluttered personal life and flourishing ministry left no time
for spiritual discipline, soul care, or proper rest and recreation.
However, my longing for a saner pace and more meaningful life
had become so intense that I was willing to try anything. As I've
heard you say a thousand times, "the cheese was sliding off my
cracker."

Meanwhile your star was rising high and fast as you did
your "ragamuffin thing," jetting hither and yon, preaching,
writing books, and giving retreats. Phoning you "from out of
nowhere" and pleading for help was positive proof that I was in
a hopelessly desperate state. Answering my call and receiving me
as an honored guest was indicative of your Christlikeness. If you
ever imagined that by welcoming me you might be "entertaining
an angel unaware," it didn't take long for you to realize, "Nope.
Not this guy."

Humbly you embraced me with unbridled kindness and
care, thus opening the way for me to expose the hidden but
real condition of my twisted and deformed soul. Tirelessly you
listened to my confession, and without my knowing, the healing
of my image of God began. Your unconditional acceptance of
me imbued me with uncommon courage to imagine that God
accepted me too. Slowly I began to experience Jesus' relentless

tenderness and care. Your persistent emphasis on Abba's scandal-
ous love initiated my slow recovery from despair.

Today I recognize that if we are fortunate enough, there
comes a time when we encounter someone who will leave an
indelible mark on our life. Someone whose character embodies
the fruits of a deep spiritual walk and whose intimacy with Jesus
is so infectious that we long to emulate it. You have been that
person in my life.

Your friendship has been like the refreshing shade of a
vast tree in the noonday heat. You've provided my soul with a
safe harbor, a sanctuary of protection. You've been a dispenser of
hope, a ward against depression, and the cause of countless belly
laughs. Most of all you've never wanted anything from me except
that I am myself.

I am your eternally grateful friend.

                                                                Fil

Dear Brennan,

  It is impossible for me to imagine the last forty years of
my life without our friendship. Your spoken message and your
writings would have made a difference, but it was the personal
friendship that made the big difference. It was so important to
me to identify the message of truth and love with a lifestyle of
happiness, humor, and good times. We both knew and acknowledged the redemptive theology of our faith and its call for duty
and sacrifice. Our personalities, however, were made for more
than sacrifice. I think for both of us—in my case for sure—our
temperament called for joy and celebration!

  As I look back, I can see how I yearned to find such quali-
ties in a "man of God," a priest. I hit pay dirt in you. I could at
last put together "the Word" and a lifestyle that was considered
"less than" in most religious quarters. I had a lot to learn. When
we met, I could not conceive of joy and celebration without
alcohol. It was a great adventure to let alcohol go and trust that
happiness could exist without it. Now, on the other side, I see
how our friendship strengthened me. I now know that joy is what
happens when we "let go." Joy is indeed our true, natural state.
And like everything, joy is a gift.

  Since it is impossible for me to put into words what our
companionship has meant, I will simply say thank you!

                                              Your friend,
                                              Paul

ACKNOWLEDGMENTS

John Irving's brilliant novel *A Prayer for Owen Meany* contains this first-page line: "I am a Christian because of Owen Meany." If there be any brilliance in these pages, I must write a similar line: I am a writer because of:

Rick Christian, my agent at Alive Communications, has been a patient prodder to "finish the story." Dan Rich, Don Pape, and the entire creative team at David C. Cook have amazed me with the acquisition of, continued faith in, and bringing to completion of these pages. Ken Gire's initial interview sessions were essential help in completing this memoir.

Paul Sheldon, Fil Anderson, Ed and Hillery Moise, and Roslyn graciously stirred up memories of the furiously flawed good times and have loved me like I didn't deserve. The Notorious men, who know who they are, have made me a better sinner.

And my friend John.

Me with my friend John Blase

NOTES

1. Frederick Buechner, *Telling Secrets: A Memoir* (San Francisco: HarperSanFrancisco, 1991), 32–33.

2. E. B. White, *Essays of E. B. White* (New York: HarperCollins, 1977), 8.

3. Louise Glück, "Matins," *The Wild Iris* (New York: HarperCollins, 1992), 26.

4. Alice Miller, *Prisoners of Childhood* (New York: BasicBooks, 1981), vii.

5. Betty Smith, *A Tree Grows in Brooklyn* (New York: Harper Perennial, 2005), 421.

6. Ibid., 6.

7. Flannery O'Connor, "The Turkey," *Collected Works* (New York: Penguin, 1988), 752.

8. *Finding Neverland*, directed by Marc Foster, Miramax, 2004.

9. Joseph Conrad, *Lord Jim* (New York: Oxford University Press, 2008), 130.

10. Jean-Jacques Antier, *Charles de Foucauld* (San Francisco: Ignatius, 1999), 104.

11. Carlo Carretto, *Letters from the Desert* (New York: Orbis, 2002), xi.

12. Father James Kavanaugh, *A Modern Priest Looks at His Outdated Church* (Highland Park, IL: Stephen J. Nash, 1967), epilogue.

13. Ibid., 11.

14. Mary Oliver, "In Blackwater Woods," *New and Selected Poems* (Boston, Beacon, 1993), 1:177.

15. Paul Harding, *Tinkers* (New York: Bellevue Literary, 2009), 61.

16. Michael Yaconelli, *Messy Spirituality* (Grand Rapids, MI: Zondervan, 2002), 16.

17. Stephen King, "Frey's Lies," *Entertainment Weekly*, www.ew.com/ew/article/0,,1155752,00.html, par. 4 (accessed June 3, 2011).

18. Robert A. Johnson and Jerry M. Ruhl, *Balancing Heaven and Earth* (New York: HarperCollins, 1998), 173–74.

19. Brennan Manning, *The Ragamuffin Gospel* (Sisters, OR: Multnomah, 1990), 31–32.

20. Fil Anderson, *Breaking the Rules* (Downers Grove, IL: InterVarsity, 2010), 80–81.

21. Robert Farrar Capon, *The Romance of the Word* (Grand Rapids, MI: Eerdmans, 1995), 20.

22. Kent Meyers, *Twisted Tree* (New York: Houghton Mifflin Harcourt, 2009), 234, 237–39.